Lesley Tahtakılıç & Margaret Mellor

The Kangal Dog of Turkey

Published by Margaret Mellor and Lesley Tahtakılıç

Published by Margaret Mellor and Lesley Tahtakılıç
Showsley Lodge, Towcester, Northamptonshire, United Kingdom

© Margaret Mellor and Lesley Tahtakılıç 2009

First published in 2009

Designed by Luisa Keig
Printed and bound in Great Britain by the MPG Books Group, Bodmin and King's Lynn

A catalogue record for this book is available from the British Library

ISBN 978 0 9563482 0 3

Contents

Preface

In bringing you the story of the Kangal Dog of Turkey, our aim has been to document a unique breed which for various reasons is facing an uncertain future.

A number of books about the Kangal have been written by Turkish authors in response to interest in the breed in its homeland, where this dog is regarded with pride as a national icon. Some of these books have been translated into English. However, being originally written for a Turkish audience they tend to neglect the broader picture of the dog's environment, which readers in other countries may not have experienced in person. We have attempted to address this need in our book.

It has been our privilege to learn about Kangal Dogs at first hand, from villagers in Sivas province who own and work with them and who have welcomed us into their homes to talk about them. Scientists, historians, and farmers abroad have shared their knowledge too, enabling us to produce a book, not specifically for dog lovers, but for anyone interested in animals, in Turkey, and in Turkish culture.

Researching and writing this book has been a labour of love. In it we pay tribute to a breed that occupies a particular niche in time and place: shaped by ancient civilizations in the region, the Kangal Dog has a role in the ecology of the modern day. It is admired the world over, yet at the same time misrepresented and exploited; a courageous protector by nature, it is itself endangered. We hope that our account will bring about a greater understanding and appreciation of this very special breed and of its homeland, Turkey.

L.T. & M.M.

Introducing the Kangal Dog

Hoş geldiniz! Welcome to the world of the Kangal Dog, the famous companion of the Turkish shepherd and guardian of his flocks.

For centuries this dog has played a vital part in the working lives of country people in the Sivas province of central Turkey. The generations have imprinted not only its striking physical characteristics but its unique behavioural qualities. The Kangal Dog (also called the Sivas-Kangal shepherd dog) is valued for its courage and strength, its loyalty to the shepherd, and its devotion to the animals in its charge, a special reputation that has long been appreciated in farming communities within and beyond the provincial borders.

But times are changing in Turkey. Young people leave their villages to build a different future; some return in later years and the traditional way of life evolves as new ideas and technologies are introduced. What does the future hold for the Kangal Dog?

The homeland of the Kangal Dog

Anatolia (*Anadolu* in Turkish) is the name given to the Asian region of Turkey, once called Asia Minor, which extends from the Caucasus in the east to the Aegean Sea in the west and from the Black Sea in the north to the Mediterranean Sea in the south.

The central Anatolian plateau is a vast, formidable expanse of mountain and steppe, embracing the modern capital, Ankara, and stretching eastwards. It is more than three times the size of the British Isles, penetrated by relatively few modern roads and only sparsely populated.

In the dry central plains, crops can be grown only in the valleys along the line of rivers which dwindle to a trickle in summer. Grazing is too sparse and the terrain and weather generally too harsh for cattle, and so the mainstay of the economy and village life is sheep rearing. Wool plays a vital part in Turkey's textiles industry and is of course the raw material for one of the country's most famous products: its carpets.

Flocks grazing on the mountainside near Serinyayla, where Turgut Özer (right) works with his dogs

It has been estimated that Turkey has over 25 million sheep (2005), and most of them are reared on these vast open plains. The flocks range over huge areas browsing on the scrubby grass and at nightfall, if the grazing is not too far distant from the shepherd's village, they are brought back to the area around the settlements, where they are less susceptible to attack by predators. If they are further away, then they have to be guarded overnight on the mountainside.

In many regions shepherds employ the ancient system of transhumance, where whole flocks, and often most of the population of the village to which they belong, migrate to summer pastures (*yaylalar*) and back with the changing seasons. Life is hard for the Turkish shepherd, and his livelihood depends to a great extent on one valuable asset: his dog.

All over Asiatic Turkey, large, strong dogs are used by the shepherds to protect their sheep. The dogs' role is to watch for the approach of danger, which can be in the form of predatory wolves, jackals, eagles or even bears and wildcats, and to place themselves between that threat and the flock. The dogs are also used to escort the sheep on their frequent treks to and from water and pasture, a task that an experienced dog will sometimes perform without the supervision of the shepherd.

The dogs that carry out these tasks are called *çoban köpekleri*: shepherd dogs. This is not the name of a breed: it simply describes the work they do. But over the centuries a number of specific types of dog have evolved into uniform populations breeding to type. This has been influenced both by human intervention—selection for particular working characteristics in the dog—and by the geographical isolation and environmental conditions of particular regions. The Kangal Dog of central Turkey is one of these breeds.

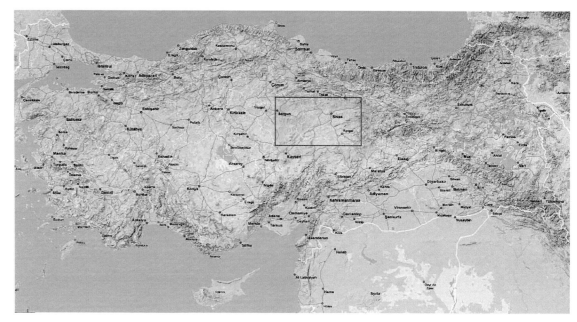

Traditional home territory of the working Kangal Dog

In this book ...

Here is a preview of the topics you can read about in the chapters that follow.

The historical setting

The history of the Kangal Dog is possibly as long as the history of Anatolia, which stretches back for thousands of years. In the Neolithic Age, Anatolia was the centre of an agricultural revolution, when animals, including dogs, were first domesticated and people began to live in the world's first farming settlements such as that excavated at Çatalhöyük in the south central region.

Anatolia was then populated by a succession of different peoples at different periods. In central Anatolia these peoples included the Hittites, Phrygians, Celts (the Galatians), Lydians, Persians, Macedonians, Romans, Arabs, Byzantines, Armenians, and finally the Turks. Branches of the Silk Road from China crossed Anatolia, as did the Persian Royal Road, a 'pony express' system of the Achaemenid Empire in the 5th century BCE. Many of these historical factors have left their mark on the city and province of Sivas, including the Kangal district, where today everyday life goes on among reminders of these ancient civilizations.

Origins

There has been much discussion in Turkey and elsewhere about the origins of the Kangal Dog. Theorists have generally assumed an exotic origin—from outside Anatolia and from various points of the compass including Mesopotamia in the south-east, Europe in the north-west, and Central Asia in the east. However, it is clear from archaeological evidence that dogs existed in Anatolia at least as long ago as 5000 BCE. So it is highly likely that there were indigenous dogs in central Anatolia when Turkic tribes began migrating into the region from Asia in the 11th century with their flocks of sheep and their own flock-guarding dogs. Flock guardians similar to, but not exactly the same as, Kangal Dogs are found today throughout the lands on that migration route: Iran, Azerbaijan, and the former Soviet republics of Central Asia. Comparisons of genetic material from archaeological finds and dogs alive today may soon throw some light on whether the roots of this breed are exotic, indigenous or both.

A Hittite statue of a lion, unearthed from Havuz village in Kangal district and now exhibited in Ankara's Museum of Anatolian Civilizations

Detail of an ivory box from the 2nd millennium BCE, also displayed in the Museum of Anatolian Civilizations

Nature, adaptation, type

As a 'landrace' breed, the Kangal Dog has evolved naturally over many generations to fit the specific environment of its central Anatolian homeland. The high, wide, open steppe of Sivas province is to a certain extent cut off from surrounding areas by rugged mountain ranges. Seasonal temperature extremes and sparse vegetation mean that to live and thrive in this area animals have had to adapt in order to withstand the tough physical conditions. The Kangal Dog has developed a number of special traits which enable it to survive and work in this harsh, remote environment. Apart from its large, strong build, other features of the dog's physique have evolved in particularly advantageous ways. Its resemblance to the local black-faced Kangal Akkaraman sheep, in size and colouring, is another characteristic that probably helps it in its working role.

Until recently there was no formalized Turkish standard to describe any of the country's dog breeds, whether hunting dogs or guarding dogs, although there is written evidence that some selective breeding of shepherd dogs has been going on for centuries. On the whole, as with horses and other livestock, animal owners have traditionally maintained their own unofficial, unwritten standards. While in the 1970s and 1980s written breed specifications for Turkish dogs began to appear in other countries, it was not until 2005 that a comprehensive breed standard for the Kangal Dog was drawn up and presented by Turkish experts.

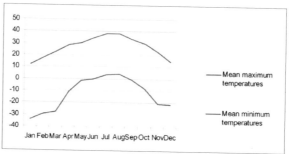

Mean minimum and maximum temperatures in Sivas, 1961–1990
Source: World Meteorological Organization (2009)

Kangals at work

The temperament and behaviour of the Kangal Dog are as important as its physical characteristics. A good shepherd dog has to be steady and predictable. Working Kangal Dogs are on duty in all seasons, at all hours. Often unseen, their place during the day is a quiet station either in the midst of the flock or on the hillside overlooking it. But nightfall sees an increase in activity as the dogs, working in pairs or teams, begin to patrol their territory, signalling their presence with a bark to each other and to any predator that may be lurking. Should any form of threat appear, the Kangal's protective instincts immediately come into play. Without hesitation the dog will place itself between the flock and that threat, be it a wolf, feral dog or other animal, or an unfamiliar human being. Using a system of different barks the dogs warn off the intruder. If necessary one or more of the team will chase it away, always leaving at least one dog to watch the flock.

In Turkey, Kangals learn how to manage and guard their sheep and goats by a canine apprenticeship system; on-the-job training happens automatically as youngsters work alongside older, experienced dogs. In countries outside Turkey, farmers have developed techniques that help their dogs to 'bond' with the stock. Whether at home or abroad, the Kangal's innate guarding ability is invaluable to the shepherd.

Life in Kangal country

As an integral part of the village and farming environment of the region, the day-to-day role of the Kangal Dog is naturally influenced by changes in that environment. Life in the countryside still follows traditional patterns, dictated mainly by the seasons and by the Moslem religion, whether of the Sunni or Alevi branch. Social life and entertainment generally centre on family events such as weddings and circumcisions, religious ceremonies, and the Kangal Festival, a celebration for the whole district, which takes place each year in July. The attractions of urban life have drawn many people away from the countryside.

The local economy in this harsh natural environment is similarly limited. From ancient times until today, farmers here have produced cereal crops and raised livestock, especially sheep. In recent years flock numbers have gradually been declining for various reasons and this constitutes a threat to the survival of the Kangal Dog in its traditional role. However, various initiatives are in place to support rural development in which it is hoped the Kangal Dog will have a part to play.

Shepherdess Ayşe Yıldırım with her flock of lambs

Kangal Dogs in Belgium

Celebrating Children's Day in Turkish style

Kangals abroad

After being 'discovered' by visitors to Turkey in the latter part of the 20th century, Kangal Dogs have made their mark in other countries. Initially kept as companions or for show, they later became appreciated for their qualities as working livestock guardians in countries where they could perform their traditional function. Their instinctive attachment to the sheep and goats placed in their care has brought the dogs worldwide recognition as an effective, non-lethal deterrent against a range of predators: coyotes and mountain lions in the USA, wild dogs and foxes in Australia, lynx and bears in Scandinavia, and most recently cheetahs in Africa.

Over the years Turkish migrant workers have brought their dogs with them to countries in western Europe, particularly Germany and Holland, and there are now small breeding populations of Kangals outside Turkey. As yet, very few national kennel clubs recognize the breed, but groups such as the Kangal Dog Club of America have been formed to encourage interest and to act as a support network for owners.

Identity

In Turkey the Kangal Dog enjoys iconic status, featuring on postage stamps and coins and in sculpture. It is regarded as a national treasure, bred at government-controlled breeding centres and protected by law. Kangals are a popular attraction at Ankara Zoo and they are feted at festivals in Turkey and elsewhere. They have been described in travellers' tales ancient and modern, and have recently found their place in scientific studies, conferences and reference books.

The Turks are proud of their national dog and are quite clear about its identity as a specific breed. They are aware that not all shepherd dogs in Anatolia can be regarded as Kangals. However, in other countries there is some confusion about this, and a good deal of ill feeling between the 'lumpers', who regard all Turkish shepherd dogs as one breed, and the 'splitters', who recognize the Kangal Dog as a breed in its own right. This situation is mystifying to Turks, as is another question that exercises minds abroad, though not in Turkey: the name of the breed.

Health, care and ownership

The rewards of owning a Kangal Dog can be great, but so can the challenges. To be frank, this is not the breed for every owner. The special qualities of this dog have developed over centuries in its working environment of central Anatolia; a knowledge of this background should help owners to understand the needs and behaviour of their Kangal, which are likely to be rather different from those of other breeds more commonly kept as companion dogs.

Kangals are large, robust dogs with few health issues specific to the breed. Health problems for working Kangals tend to differ from those of companion dogs as a result of the marked differences in their working and living environments. In general Kangals are easy to maintain, clean in their habits and straightforward in their physical demands. Understanding the mindset of this breed, however, requires more time and effort on the part of the new owner: being 'chosen' by a Kangal is a privilege, and also a great responsibility.

Kangals are good companions for other animals in the household

The future

Changes in the socio-economic environment of Anatolia are threatening the future of the Kangal Dog in its home territory. Some feel that the continuation of the breed as a working dog will depend on finding alternative uses for its special, traditional skills. However, development initiatives have been introduced to support farmers and encourage sheep rearing and if these succeed the Kangal is likely to retain its place in the landscape of the region.

Breed type is under threat from commercial interests, especially from breeders prepared to sacrifice the innate qualities of the Kangal by hybridizing it to produce bigger dogs with more aggressive temperament. A positive development in the welfare of animals in general in Turkey, and of the Kangal Dog in particular, is the passing of the Animal Protection Law in 2004. Article 11, which forbids the pitting of animals against other live animals, is of particular relevance. The formation of a national Turkish kennel club may help to protect the identity of the different Turkish breeds and encourage a new generation of responsible dog owners. The greatest hope for the future of this breed is perhaps a general awareness, at home and abroad, that the Kangal Dog is a valuable part of Turkey's natural heritage.

Hasan Hüseyin Türkdoğan has a lifetime's experience of working with Kangal Dogs

2

The historical setting

High up on the open steppeland of central Anatolia lies the small town of Kangal in the Turkish province of Sivas. The Kangal Dog takes its name from this town and area, which is regarded in Turkey as the heartland of the breed. The history of the Kangal Dog is inextricably linked to the history of the town and region of Kangal.

The Hittites

Over thousands of years, wave upon wave of peoples have passed through or settled in this area of Anatolia. Although there were certainly earlier inhabitants of the area, archaeological evidence from Kangal villages really begins with the Hittites. The ruins of Hattusas (Boğazköy), the capital of the Hittite Empire, lie about 240 km to the west of Kangal as the crow flies. The area covered today by Sivas province was known to the Hittites as Upper Land. It is likely that Hittite peasants farmed the land in much the same way as Turkish farmers do today. Just as today, the main crops were wheat and barley, and cattle, sheep, goats, horses, donkeys and bees were kept. Farmers would have lived in flat-roofed mud brick houses, similar to those still found in Kangal villages. The Hittite farmer had a number of predators to contend with, including lions, leopards, wolves and wild boar, of which only wolves and wild boar now remain.

The Hittites used dogs for hunting and herding. Just as it does today, the presence of wild animal predators in an area of cattle, sheep and goat rearing required the use of dogs as herd and flock guards. A high value was placed upon working dogs, especially herding dogs. This is clearly demonstrated by Hittite laws stating penalties for stealing or killing animals, with almost double the penalty for herding dogs compared with hunting dogs (Bryce, 2002, 2005; Macqueen, 1975/2001).

Hittites

The Hittites were an Indo-European speaking people, who controlled a large part of Anatolia during the Bronze Age. Where they came from and when they arrived in Anatolia are questions disputed among scholars. However, it is known that from approximately 2000 BCE, people speaking Indo-European languages were living in Anatolia. Since Anatolia is most unlikely to be the 'homeland' of these languages, their speakers must have arrived from elsewhere, most probably from north of the Black Sea, between the lower Danube and the northern foothills of the Caucasus.

The Hittites established an empire that ruled much of Anatolia and Mesopotamia until their defeat by the 'Sea Peoples' in about 1200 BCE. The Hittites adopted much of the culture of the local inhabitants in the areas where they settled.

Hittite Laws

Penalties for stealing or killing animals:

bull	15 cattle	cow	6 oxen
stallion	15 horses	mare	6 horses
ram	15 sheep	ewe	6 sheep
mule	2 mules	pig	6 shekels
plough ox	10 cattle	bee hives	6 shekels
draft horse	10 cattle	plain dog	1 shekel
trained goat	10 cattle	**herding dog**	**20 shekels**
piglet	100 litres of barley	hunting dog	12 shekels

Havuz village

One of the oldest villages in the Kangal district, and a local centre for the surrounding hamlets, is Havuzköy.

This is a relatively large community, consisting of about 300 families, administered by four *muhtar*s (a *muhtar* is the elected head of a village or neighbourhood). There are currently (2008) ten Havuz flocks, each comprising 500–600 sheep, but as little as 10 years ago there were many more. One of the *muhtar*s, Halil İbrahim Yıldırım, explained that the availability of tractors to plough the upland pastures (*yaylalar*) has meant that wheat can now be grown on what was previously summer grazing.

Havuz also has a reputation for reliable Kangal Dogs of very good breed type and quality and there is a demand for puppies from this village. Despite the decline in sheep husbandry, the good local Kangal Dog bloodlines for which this village is famous have been maintained and are greatly valued.

From spring to autumn the dogs escort the flocks every morning to grazing up to 10 km from the village, returning with them at nightfall. Some flocks, however, are moved to the upland pastures in spring, where they remain until early winter, together with their shepherds and dogs. They spend the day wandering the pastures but return to barns in the *yayla* hamlets at night. In winter the flocks are held in barns and fed hay.

The Hittites used dogs for hunting and herding. Dogs are depicted in this large Hittite wall sculpture of a lion fight, from Alacahöyük (near present-day Boğazköy), c.2000 BCE. The tail carriage of one of the dogs is identical to that of a Kangal Dog. This sculpture is exhibited at the Ankara Museum of Anatolian Civilizations

One of the Kangal Dogs owned by Halil İbrahim Bey of Havuz

At Karaseki in the hills just outside Havuz lies an important Hittite site, which was excavated in the 1940s. A large basalt statue of a lion was unearthed, one of a pair that would have stood guard at each side of a Hittite city gate. It stands now in the Museum of Anatolian Civilizations in Ankara. Interestingly, the Museum keeps several Kangal Dogs to patrol the grounds and keep watch over the national heritage!

Asım Dikçal is now in his eighties but as a young lad he was part of the team of villagers who helped the archaeologists unearth the lion statue and transport it from the site by cart. 'It was so heavy that it broke the first cart and they had to get another one', he says.

Asım Dikçal, who helped with the excavation of the lion statue in the 1940s. All over Turkey, reminders of the ancient civilizations that successively populated this country continue to be part of the village scene. For generations Asım Bey's family has grazed sheep on the hills around the ancient settlement, always with Kangal Dogs to protect the flock

The splendid Hittite lion from Havuzköy (left), on display in Ankara's Museum of Anatolian Civilizations (Right) drawing water from the fountain at Doymuş hamlet on the yayla near Karaseki. The black basalt rock forming the fountainhead was once part of a Hittite structure

A jewel-studded ivory box from the Hittite city of Acemhöyük, engraved with figures of herders, livestock, dogs (of a familiar conformation) and lions, 1750–1200 BCE. This box is exhibited in the Museum of Anatolian Civilizations in Ankara

Before the Hittites

But the Hittites were probably not the first inhabitants of the Kangal area. A mysterious people known as the Hatti are mentioned in Assyrian records and are thought to have preceded the Hittites. The Turkish archaeologist Ekrem Akurgal regarded the Hatti as the native Anatolians. The 'Land of Hatti' was probably centred around modern Divriği, which lies about 50 km to the east of Kangal.

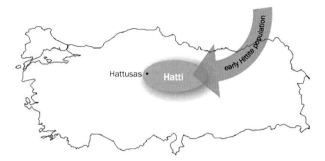

Even earlier than the Hatti, it is likely that the area was occupied and farmed from around 9000 BCE, with the domestication of crops and animals and settlement in agricultural villages.

Once the earlier hunting and gathering economy had changed to settled farming, the need arose for trade, especially for tin. Although Anatolia was rich in minerals such as gold, silver and copper, it lacked tin, needed as an alloy for copper in the production of bronze. This need was filled by Assyrian traders from the south-east, who established trading colonies, known as *karum*s, in various parts of Anatolia. The nearest *karum* to the Sivas area was at Kanesh (Kültepe) near modern Kayseri, approximately 200 km south-west of Kangal. From 1940 to 1780 BCE, Assyrian traders settled in the local communities, adopted local customs and took Anatolian wives. This appears to be a long tradition in Anatolia: newcomers settle alongside earlier inhabitants, intermarry and are absorbed into the local culture.

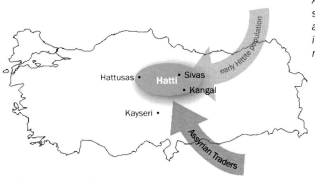

Assyrian traders set up karums around Kayseri in the second millennium BCE

In Babylonian times it was believed that the dog was related to the lion, so feline rather than canine, a notion reflected in this slightly ambiguous depiction of a large dog and its keeper. This Babylonian terracotta dates from the period of the Assyrian traders in Anatolia, 2000–1600 BCE (Imager eproduction courtesy of the Trustees of the British Museum)

After the Hittites

After the Hittites, the region now covered by the province of Sivas was ruled or settled successively by Phrygians, Lydians, Persians, Macedonians, Romans, Arabs (Ummayid), Byzantines and Armenians until Turkic tribes entered Anatolia from the east. There may even have been some Celtic influence in the 3rd century BCE, when three Galatian tribes settled in central Anatolia. One of these tribes, the Trocmi, established their capital at Tavium, which is near present-day Yozgat, about 200 km west of Kangal (Beresford-Ellis, 1990).

The arrival of the Turks

The origins of the Turks lie in Central Asia near the border with China. A Chinese record of 1328 BCE refers to a people called the Tu-kiu, a possible origin for the word Turk. The Oghuz tribe of Turks, from which the Turks of modern Turkey claim descent, believed their homeland was in the Altai mountains on the borders of modern Mongolia and Russia. They were one of many Turkic-speaking tribes living a partly settled, partly nomadic life on the Central Asian steppes. Over hundreds of years, possibly as a result of desertification, these tribes gradually moved westwards, together with their flocks, herds, horses and dogs. The main migration began with the Göktürks in the 6th century CE. Today there are peoples speaking a variety of Turkic dialects right across Central Asia and in Siberia, Moldova, southern Russia and, of course, Turkey.

British livestock expert Laurence Alderson has investigated how many breeds of farm animal may have evolved, tracing their ancestry through patterns of human migration and military conquest. He describes the Urial and Argali wild sheep of Asia, believed to have contributed to many modern, black-faced, horned breeds that are farmed throughout the world. This distinct group probably arrived in Britain from Scandinavia with the Vikings in the 8th century CE. The second millennium BCE saw the beginning of important movements of people and their flocks westwards from the Asian steppes, including direct migration into and settlement in both northern Europe and eastern Anatolia.

(Alderson, 1978)

Seljuk architecture can be seen throughout Sivas province. This 13th-century hospital at Divriği in the east is a fine example

The Seljuks

The Seljuks were one of the tribes of the Oghuz Turks. As they moved gradually westwards from Central Asia over the centuries, they developed a strong and distinctive culture. Their first powerful state was established in Persia, the Great Seljuk Empire (1037). From this time they came into contact with the Byzantine Empire in Eastern Anatolia, resulting in the Battle of Manzikert (Malazgırt) north of Lake Van in 1071. At this battle the Seljuk army, led by their sultan, Alp Arslan, routed the Byzantine army and captured the Byzantine Emperor, Romanus IV Diogenes, who was subsequently ransomed. Although marauding bands of fierce Turcoman nomads had previously been active within the Byzantine Empire, they had simply raided and retreated.

The victory at Manzikert opened the way for the establishment of the Seljuk Sultanate of Rûm (the contemporary name for the region comprising Anatolia and the Balkans). Although the capital of the sultanate was at Konya, Sivas was one of its most important cities. During their centuries-long journey towards Anatolia the Seljuks had adopted the Moslem religion and had developed a sophisticated and tolerant culture: Jewish doctors and Greek and Armenian scholars were welcomed at the Seljuk court. Mosques, seminaries, hospitals and caravanserais were built throughout the sultanate. The Sultanate of Rûm was effectively ended when the Seljuk army was routed by the Mongols at the Battle of Kuzadağ (1242) on the road between Sivas and Erzincan.

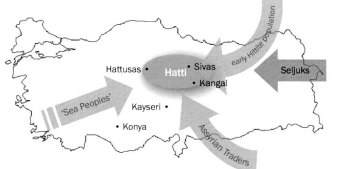

When the Seljuks arrived in Anatolia from the east, in the 11th century, Sivas became an important centre in the Sultanate of Rûm

The Silk Road

Another important factor in the history of the region is the fact that ancient trade routes linking Europe to China, known collectively as the Silk Road, and the Persian Royal Road both crossed this part of Anatolia. The provincial capital, Sivas, was an important crossroads on the caravan routes from Persia and from Baghdad.

Camel caravans laden with silk, spices, minerals and other valuable products would stop over at the caravanserais or *han*s (inns) which were built at intervals along the Silk Road to provide secure shelter for travellers and their animals. More than 130 of these massive structures were built during the Seljuk era, of which only about 40—generally, those that have remained in use over the centuries—are still standing today. Efforts are being made to protect the Seljuk caravanserais and the Turkish government aims to have all remaining *han*s restored by 2010.

Alacahan

The Alacahan caravanserai stands 25 km from Kangal town. It is a large building constructed of alternate dark- and light-coloured stone blocks, the appearance of which gives it its name: *alaca* = speckled, *han* = inn. It is said to have been built in 1231 by the Seljuk Sultan Alaadin Keykubad I.

This *han* has been in more or less constant use over the years, both as a working caravanserai for travelling merchants and as a social and cultural meeting place. A thriving village has grown up around it; every year the Alacahan is one of the main venues in the celebration of the Kangal Festival and the Second International Kangal Dog Symposium of July 2005 was held in this historic building.

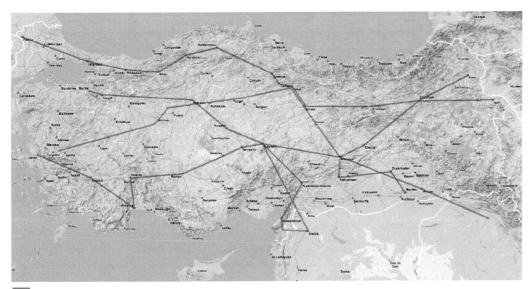

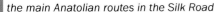 *the main Anatolian routes in the Silk Road*

the Persian Royal Road

The Epic of Ergenekon

Once upon a time in Central Asia, a powerful Turkish tribe, led by Kağan II Han, was overthrown in an uprising by its subject peoples. The only Turkish survivors of the battle were Kağan II Han's son, Kaya, and his nephew, Dokuz Oğuz Görkem, and their wives. Gathering their herds and flocks, they fled into the high mountains. After a perilous journey through steep rocky defiles, they reached an astonishing place in the heart of the mountains, a place where streams flowed, birds sang and there were all kinds of plants, fruits and animals. They called this place Ergenekon.

There they settled, tended their flocks and multiplied. With each new birth a grey wolf appeared on the rocks and bayed the glad tidings to the moon. Over hundreds of years the population expanded until Ergenekon became overcrowded. The Turks had never forgotten their homeland beyond the mountains and they decided to return there. But how could all these people pass through the seemingly impregnable mountains?

An ironworker came up with a solution. 'There's a deep seam of iron in this mountain,' he said. 'If we melt the metal it will create a passage.' So they built a huge fire on the mountainside and fanned it with seven huge bellows. The mountain became as red as a pomegranate, the iron melted and a passage opened up through the mountain. In the moonlight a wide plain could be seen through the passage.

On the high rocks a blue-maned grey wolf appeared, howling at the moon. The wolf started walking through the passage and the people followed. The wolf led the Turks out of Ergenekon back to their ancestral homeland on the steppes.

(Özdemir, 2006)

The Turks and wolves

By the time the Turks arrived in Anatolia the main livestock predator was the wolf, lions and leopards having largely disappeared from the region. The Turkish peoples have historically had an ambivalent attitude to wolves. On the one hand the wolf is seen as a predator, so farmers keep large dogs such as the Kangal to protect their flocks. On the other hand the wolf appears in myths and legends as a founder and saviour of the Turkish peoples.

The Gökturks, who lived in what is now the Chinese province of Xinjiang, believed that they were descended from a she-wolf. According to their mythology, the inhabitants of a Turkic village were massacred by Chinese soldiers. However, a small baby survived, to be found and nursed by an old blue-maned she-wolf named Asena. Later the wolf gave birth to half-wolf, half-human cubs, who founded the Ashina clan from which the Gökturks descended.

Few people in modern Turkey appear to be familiar with the Asena myth, although baby girls are sometimes given the name Asena. The epic of Ergenekon, however, in which the heroic action of a wolf is also described, is well known (Talbot Rice, 1961).

Today wolves still prey on the sheep, goats and cattle grazing on the central Anatolian steppe, but rather than hunting down and killing the wolves, the villagers prefer to use their shepherd dogs to warn the wolves off, allowing wolves, people and livestock to live in harmony.

A crossroads of civilizations

This chapter provides only a glimpse of the rich fabric of Anatolian history, but it has given insights into the range of cultures and peoples that swept across the country before the rise of the Ottoman Empire in 1300 CE. As each wave of new arrivals appeared, they tended to settle beside the earlier inhabitants, intermarry and adopt local customs. Regardless of the ruling class of the time, throughout the millennia it is likely that the inhabitants of the Sivas-Kangal region simply carried on living and farming in the time-honoured fashion of their ancestors, much as they do today.

Landowners and villagers have continued to farm the land, growing cereal crops and raising their sheep, goats, cattle and poultry. And to protect their animals from predators they will always have had their flock-guarding dogs.

A rich heritage

When the German archaeologist Hans Henning von der Osten was presented to Mustafa Kemal Atatürk at a reception in the 1930s, Atatürk congratulated him on excavating the remains of the ancestors of the Turks at the Hittite capital at Boğazköy. Some people smiled at this remark, thinking it was foolish. The inhabitants of modern Turkey are proud of their roots in Central Asia. Others, however, have registered their agreement with Atatürk, among them Professor Richard N. Frye, Agha Khan Professor Emeritus of Iranian Studies and founder of the Center for Middle Eastern Studies, Harvard University.

... in my opinion he was quite correct, for the ancestors of the people of the Turkish Republic are a blend of those who always lived in Anatolia and the nomads who came from Central Asia and gave their language to everyone. The heritage of both Anatolia and Central Asia belongs to the heritage of the present-day inhabitants of Turkey.

(Frye, in Çağatay and Kuban, 2006)

Origins

Where do Kangal Dogs come from? Various theories have been put forward in response to this question. Could they have come into Anatolia from the south, from Mesopotamia? Or with the Turkic tribes as they migrated west from Central Asian countries? Or are they indigenous to central Anatolia? It has even been suggested that they came from Europe with the Celtic tribes in the 3rd century BCE. And a local legend in the village of Deliktaş relates that Kangal Dogs are all descended from a dog, or dogs, that went absent without leave from the Ottoman army while passing through the vicinity.

The domestication of dogs

Domestication of dogs is believed to have taken place about 15,000 years ago. Recent genetic research by a Swedish team, led by Dr Peter Savolainen, strongly suggests that domestication took place in East Asia. It has even been claimed that all dogs in the world descend from three females near China (Savolainen *et al.*, 2002). Researchers believe that dogs were among the first animals to be domesticated and that they co-evolved with humans. Evidence for this is provided by recent studies in dog cognition. Dogs are able to understand non-verbal signals from humans, such as pointing to a hidden food source. One study showed that even very young puppies that had had no human contact, were able to do this, whereas wolves raised by humans did not have these skills. This indicates that dogs evolved in a mixed-species environment: they had to deal with human society as well as dog society, so dogs that could read both human and dog signals were selected for survival in the evolutionary process (Hare *et al.*, 2002; Hare and Tomasello, 2005).

Domesticated dogs in Anatolia

Definitive archaeological evidence of domesticated dogs in Anatolia was found at a site at Van-Yoncatepe Castle in eastern Turkey. There, in an Urartian necropolis dating from 1000 BCE, 15 dog skeletons (13 male, one female, one unknown) were found, buried alongside human remains.

Detailed examination of the dog skeletons, carried out by researchers at the Veterinary Faculty of Istanbul University, indicated that these dogs were of medium size (with a height at the withers of 50–55 cm) and were probably used for hunting or for guarding livestock. Measurement of the skulls revealed that they were of the dolichocephalic (long-headed) type (Onar *et al.*, 2002), so these may have been hounds.

Very little else is known about the appearance of these Urartian dogs. Hunting and stock breeding were vital to the Urartian economy in what was then a heavily wooded area rich in prey, and working dogs would therefore have had great importance in that society. Evidence from the skeletons suggests that the dogs were not kept as pets but were kept outdoors and had a generally poor diet.

Professor Vedat Onar of Istanbul University and Urartu skeletons of a man and a dog, from 3000 years ago

Part of a transcript of one of the wall paintings from Level V at Çatalhöyük: herds of livestock on the plain of Aksaray, with volcanoes behind them (Mellaart, 1999) (Image reproduction courtesy of James Mellaart and Cornucopia magazine)

Ancient depictions of dogs

Although no representations of Urartian dogs have been discovered, depictions of dogs have been found at other Anatolian archaeological sites as well as in the neighbouring areas, although it is not always clear whether these dogs were domesticated.

Excavations of a prehistoric farming village at Jarmo, east of Kirkuk in present day Iraq, unearthed a number of small clay figurines representing dogs (6000–5400 BCE). These have been described as having 'jaunty upcurled tails, uncharacteristic of any wolf' and as being 'the earliest definitive evidence of the development of "man's best friend"' (Izady, 1993; Houghton Brodrick, 1972). Although very primitive, they do give some idea of the appearance of dogs in the region at that time, the most notable feature being the upcurled tail.

Archaeology at the Neolithic settlement of Çatalhöyük in south central Anatolia has provided a clearer depiction of dogs, in hunting scenes.

Çatalhöyük

Near the Turkish city of Konya in south central Anatolia lie the ruins of the first known town in the world. Named after the 80-metre high mound under which it was discovered, Çatalhöyük (fork mound) goes back 9000 years. In this oldest and largest of Neolithic centres, around 10,000 inhabitants lived in small mud-brick houses built close together and entered via the roof. They were some of the world's first settled people—farmers who grew wheat, barley, lentils and chickpeas, herders who tended sheep, goats, cattle and pigs, and traders who sold obsidian, a hard, black volcanic glass. The walls of some houses were plastered and painted with scenes of life in and around the town at various periods, giving an amazing insight into this prehistoric society. There were also scenes of other landscapes in the Mediterranean and Aegean areas.

A Hittite curse

Hittite curse formulas were warnings to people who might steal, damage or destroy something such as a monument. A long curse formula ending one Hittite pictographic inscription contains a clear picture of a dog. It is impossible to judge the size of the dog, although if large it would bear a remarkable resemblance to a modern Kangal. The curse reads '**... and let the dogs of Nikarawas eat away his head ...**'.

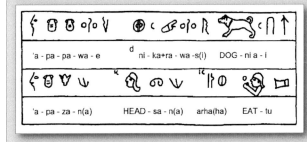

Theories about the origin of Kangal Dogs

It is clear from ancient representations that domesticated dogs with some similarities to the Kangal Dog, in particular the upcurled tail, existed in Anatolia and nearby areas thousands of years ago. However, it is unclear whether any of these dogs could have developed into the Kangal Dog of today. Various claims have been made as to the origin of Kangals, some of which are more credible than others.

One commonly held belief is that they came into Anatolia from the south-east, from Mesopotamia. This theory seems to be based on Assyrian reliefs of about 650 BCE, showing large powerful-looking dogs in lion hunting scenes. However, Kangals are not hunting dogs. Their instinct is to guard flocks and warn off predators, not to hunt down and kill them. Furthermore, if they were native to Mesopotamia—modern Iraq, Syria, Lebanon, Egypt and southern Anatolia—we would expect to find Kangal-type dogs in that area today, which is not the case. In addition, the dogs shown in the reliefs, though of a similar size to Kangals, are heavier in build, with squarer heads and straightish rather than curled tails. They appear to be of a more mastiff type.

Powerful dogs were used by the court of King Ashurbanipal for hunting lions and wild asses (Nineveh, 645–635 BCE) (Image reproduction courtesy of the Trustees of the British Museum)

Another suggestion is that Kangals arrived in Anatolia with Celtic mercenaries from Europe in the 3rd century BCE, as the so-called 'dogs of the Galatians'. This view is presented in booklets issued by the Turkish Ministry of Culture and Tourism (2008) and can be found on Celtic web sites. The theory seems to be based on a belief that the name, Kangal, derives from a Celtic language (*kan* = dog and *gal* = Galatian) and the fact that the Trocmi tribe settled not far to the west of the Sivas-Kangal area. However, the Galatians were a war-like people who arrived in Anatolia as mercenaries, not as herdsmen, so it seems unlikely that they brought flocks with dogs.

A local legend associated with the village of Deliktaş, on the Old Silk Road near Kangal, relates that the breed was started by a dog that escaped from the Ottoman army when it was passing through the district. The dog in question was said to have been presented to the Ottoman Sultan (Yavuz Sultan Selim or Murat IV) by an Indian Maharajah. This Indian dog had greatly impressed the sultan by fighting and killing a lion at the palace. Presumably it was this aggressive behaviour which led to its being drafted into the Ottoman army.

An even more outlandish legend claims that the Kangal was derived from the lion and tiger during the Assyrian and Babylonian periods. This myth may have developed because of the lioness-like appearance of Kangal dogs on the move, together with the belief at that period that dogs were feline, and therefore related to lions and other big cats.

The royal hunting mastiffs

These five little clay models (about 5 cm high by 7 cm long) are part of a set of ten, two painted in each of five colours, that were ritually stationed on either side of the door of Ashurbanipal's North Palace at Nineveh. They were substitutes for real-life guarding dogs and are described by Curtis and Reade (2005) as 'mastiffs of the royal hunting breed'.

The name of each dog is inscribed in cuneiform on its side. They translate (from top left) as: 'Don't think, bite!', 'Catcher of the enemy', 'Biter of his foe', 'Expeller of evil' and 'Loud is his bark'.

These models are also thought to have been the artist's prototypes for the dogs in the great Assyrian wall sculptures in the North Palace. However, these dogs seem to have curled or docked tails. They are now part of the British Museum collection.

The most credible theory?

Perhaps the most credible of the Kangal origin theories is that proposed by Professor Hüseyin Karadağ of the Veterinary Faculty of Yüzüncü Yıl University in Van in eastern Turkey. In his paper, 'An investigation on the opinions on the place name of Kangal and the origin of Kangal Dog' (2002), he asserts that the dog came to Anatolia after 1071 CE with the Kangli clan of Turks and their flocks during their migration from Central Asia. The fact that similar flock-guarding dogs are still found today on the Central Asian steppes is presented by supporters of this theory as clear proof. It is certainly true that animal husbandry was, and is, an essential component of the lifestyle of the nomadic peoples of Central Asia as shown in the photograph that opens this chapter, taken in Kirghizstan. Since land is not privately owned in nomadic societies, wealth is expressed by the ownership of flocks and herds and this was true of the ancient Turks. To protect this wealth from all kinds of predators, guard dogs were a necessary precaution.

Most people would agree with Professor Karadağ in dismissing the Deliktaş story as unscientific—even more so the idea that Kangals are the descendants of lions or tigers. These can be viewed as simply myths. For the same reasons, the theories about Mesopotamian and Galatian origin also seem hard to support.

Indigenous, exotic or both?

So, did the Kangal Dog arrive fully formed in the Kangal district, together with the Kangli tribe and their sheep? It seems probable that the various clans and tribes gradually moving westwards into Anatolia over the centuries did arrive with their flocks and shepherd dogs. But it is unclear how far their dogs resembled the flock-guarding dogs of Anatolia today—the Kangal, the Akbaş, the Kars Dog and others.

Speculation as to the origins of the Kangal Dog tends to fall into two categories, that the breed is indigenous to the Sivas-Kangal region, or that it is exotic, from outside the region. But the picture is not necessarily so black and white. It is quite possible that the Kangal Dog of today is the descendant of both indigenous and exotic forebears.

The history of the region is very long. Chapter 2 has described how successive waves of different peoples moved into the area and, while regimes may have changed, the people themselves, the villagers, tended to carry on with their life on the land, intermarrying with the newcomers. It is also at least possible that sheep brought by the newcomers interbred with the sheep of the local people. And that their shepherd dogs also interbred with the local shepherd dogs. Theoretically, the Kangal Dog of today could carry genes from the dogs of the Hittites, Phrygians, Lydians, Persians, Macedonians, Romans, Arabs, Byzantines and Armenians as well as the Turks. Only by comparing the genetic profile of today's dogs and canine remains recovered from archaeological studies will it be possible to build up an accurate picture.

DNA studies

At the Middle East Technical University in Ankara, Dr Evren Koban and her colleagues carried out studies using DNA samples from various types of Turkish dog: Kangal, Akbaş, Tazı (the Turkish Saluki) and free-living dogs (Altunok *et al.*, 2005). The aim of this research was to establish that the dogs could be genetically differentiated into separate breeds by the use of molecular markers (microsatellites). The study successfully proved this.

In later work (Koban *et al.*, 2008), researchers pooled mitochondrial DNA samples from Turkish dogs and other Eurasian dogs to gain a better understanding not only of the genetic relationship between Kangal and Akbaş dogs but of their links to the dogs of other countries. The findings indicated that the forebears of the Kangal and Akbaş may have followed different migration routes from Asia, at different periods in history. South-west Asian dogs (from Afghanistan, Uzbekistan, Tadjikistan, and Kazakhstan) were found to be the closest to the Kangal Dogs, and the degree of genetic diversity in the Kangal also suggested that some introgression by various types of European wolf took place along its migration route.

Scientists are working on the next phase in the genetic investigation of the Kangal Dog: to compare its DNA with genetic material recovered from canine bones found at Çatalhöyük. This might provide clues as to whether the Kangal is descended from the first domesticated dogs in Anatolia.

Koochee dog of Afghanistan

Alabai dog of Turkmenistan

During research for his PhD on the Kangal Dog, Dr Orhan Yılmaz photographed many flock-guarding dogs in Northern Afghanistan, Turkmenistan and Iran. Some of these dogs do, indeed, bear a resemblance to Kangals, as shown here (Yılmaz, 2007). However, the variability of coat colour and conformation in most of these working dogs signals other influences in their development

Nature, adaptation, type

Throughout the natural world, species have evolved to seek the best possible fit with the physical environment in which they live. This is as true for the largest of mammals as it is for the smallest microorganisms.

The camel, famously, is designed to withstand dehydration and even to vary its own body temperature to suit external conditions; its broad, strong feet enable it to travel the long distances between water sources across sand that would defeat other animals. At the other extreme, parasites and even viruses have developed life cycles that maintain an equilibrium with their particular hosts, their habitat and the seasons. In all cases the aim is to survive and thereby to ensure the succession of the next generation.

Take a step down from the species level and the picture becomes even more interesting. Ever since humans began to raise livestock for food or other products, it has been known that, for example, certain types of sheep will thrive on unlikely kinds of pasture (for example seaweed); that buffalo from some regions are more tractable as draught animals than those from others; that there are breeds of indigenous livestock, such as fell sheep in northern Britain, with unusual tolerance of extreme weather conditions. Studies of cattle in sub-Saharan Africa (such as Murray and Njogu, 1989) have shown that certain old breeds have innate resistance to trypanosomosis (a devastating disease transmitted by tsetse flies) and that this resistance is greatest in the breeds with the longest local history, traceable over some 7000 years.

The unique value of these special breeds—their genetic diversity and its capacity to hold the answer to the future needs of their species—has been recognized by organizations such as the Rare Breeds

The significance of breeds

A breed can basically be viewed as a predictable genetic package. ... Livestock guardian dogs are a fascinating genetic resource of great value and utility, and safeguarding them as breeds is of vital concern to dog breeders as well as agriculturalists. Having these as predictable genetic packages is essential to a host of livestock owners. Livestock guardian dogs need to be consistent and predictable in order for the livestock industry to have rational choices for different situations. Different dogs are needed for different situations, and this is where breeds and breeders come in.

Landrace breeds

The term 'landrace' refers to domesticated animals or plants that have developed their breed type from generations of adaptation to a combination of function and the demands of their particular natural, physical and cultural environment.

They have evolved naturally, with minimal assistance or guidance from humans, to develop stable, heritable physical and behavioural characteristics. There is, however, more variation in the appearance of landrace animals than in the more highly bred (inbred), formalized breeds of which they often form the basis.

(Sponenberg, 1998)

Compared to adult wolves, the adult dog, in many breeds, retains characteristics typical of the young of wolves, who are more social and less dominant than their parents. Again in contrast to wolves, many adult dogs display such physical characteristics as soft fluffy coats, round bodies, large heads and eyes, and pendant ears (Vilà et al., 1997). These characteristics are common to many young mammals and tend to encourage protective and nurturing behaviour from adult mammals, humans included. Selection for these characteristics may be deliberate or inadvertent.

Depending on the desired type of behaviour, different dog breeds are differently neotenized, that is, they retain different juvenile characteristics. Flock-guarding dogs, such as the Kangal, are said to retain the most juvenile characteristics.

• They stay close to their 'litter', for example their flock of sheep.

• They display very little predatory behaviour, being bred to protect sheep, a natural prey, rather than prey on them.

• When they feel threatened they bark and try to alert the dominant members of their pack, attacking as a last resort.

Flock-guarding dogs also tend to retain many juvenile physical characteristics such as a soft coat and pendant ears. The sheep they are guarding are not intimidated by these features, but they would be by the physical appearance of a dog with more wolf-like features.

Perhaps this also explains the similarity in appearance between successful shepherd dogs and their sheep. Kangal sheep and Kangal Dogs are similar in size and colour (including the black muzzle) with pendant ears and tail. It may be that dogs which resembled their sheep were more successful in relating to the flock, being less intimidating to them, and were therefore preferred by the owners when it came to breeding successive generations.

Survival Trust in the United Kingdom, the American Livestock Breeds Conservancy and the Rare Breeds Conservation Society of New Zealand. However, such organizations are mainly concerned with production livestock; the working dogs that have also evolved over thousands of years to protect them have received less attention.

The origin of dogs and the beginnings of breeds

The long debate about the ancestry of the domestic dog, *Canis familiaris*, and its links to other species such as the jackal, has moved forward significantly with the arrival of DNA analysis. Genetic studies now lead scientists to conclude that the domestic dog evolved from the wolf (*Canis lupus*), although the date of divergence of the two species is much less certain. It is generally believed that wolf and dog species split approximately 15,000 years ago, although some researchers suggest a much more distant origin (Savolainen *et al.*, 2002).

As in some other species, this evolution involved a process called paedomorphism or neoteny, the retention of juvenile characteristics in the mature animal. Selection for these characteristics contributed to the development of a range of breeds, from companion dogs to working types including the shepherd dogs.

Kangal and flock at the roadside near Ulaş: size and other physical characteristics are similar

Adaptation in the Kangal Dog

Whatever the origins of the Kangal Dog—and the most likely influences from ancient times have been explored in the earlier chapters of this book—there can be no doubt that geography and climate have played a major part in the development of a distinct and recognizable regional breed.

The topography of the Sivas area on the map shows that the homeland of the Kangal Dog is bounded by formidable mountain ranges, and the high upland between them, at an elevation of 1500–1700 metres, is exposed steppe on which sheep range. Given the natural boundaries, it is not surprising that there has been little natural infiltration by other landrace breeds over time. (Introduction via human migration is, of course, a different phenomenon.) This is not a small area, either. For people unfamiliar with Turkey it is easy to forget just how large a country it is; Sivas province alone is rather larger than, for example, Wales or the US state of Massachusetts, and not much smaller than Belgium.

Impression from the cylinder seal of Bel-Bin (c.600 BCE), a Babylonian shepherd, showing the 'good protecting dog' with livestock. This seal is in the Musée de la Porte de Hal, Brussels

Shepherd dogs: the 'good protecting dog'

Geologist and archaeologist Raphael Pumpelly (1837–1923) carried out excavations of 6000-year-old Turkmen settlements at Anau, on the southern border of Turkmenistan, in 1903 and 1904. Pumpelly looked at the distinction made, even in ancient times, between different breeds of dog: the physical characteristics and behavioural traits that made them suitable for different roles in society.

If … we would look for the shepherd-dog of the East, which might possibly have derived from the dog of Anau, we must turn our eyes to where the earliest rays of the light of history penetrate the prehistoric darkness—to Babylon, Assyria and Egypt.

The Assyrian monuments do not introduce us to more than two varieties of the dog—the large and powerful mastiff used in the chase of great animals, and the grayhound used in coursing the hare. Other breeds, however, were doubtless known to the inhabitants of Assyria and Babylonia. In the bilingual lists which give all words in Accadian and Assyrian, we find the Assyrian word na-adh-ru, 'the protecting dog' with the Accadian equivalent sega which probably means 'the good mouth-opening dog'; then follows the Assyrian cab-bi-luv, from 'to tie up' or 'chain up', represented by the same lik-ka-gab-a. Houghton, who gives these translations, thinks that na-adh-ru and cab-bi-luv both stand for some strong dog, which was used both as a watch-dog to guard the house and as a shepherd-dog to guard the flocks. The idea embodied in … 'the chained-up mouth-opening dog' answers well to a house-dog; and the notion conveyed by … 'the good protecting dog' is quite descriptive of the same kind of dog when used as a shepherd-dog.

One of the best representations of 'the good protecting dog' is on the cylinder seal of Bel-Bin. This dog seems to be of a large, powerful breed, with his tail rolled up and his ears drooping down. Another shepherd-dog is represented on a cylinder-seal of the Clercq collection. The other dogs of the Babylonians and Assyrians were all intended for the chase, from the very large mastiff to the swift grayhound.

Even to-day one still finds in those regions, extending as far as Asia Minor, a large shepherd-dog … used, as was the case among the Assyrians, to guard houses and protect the flocks from wild animals. One can form some idea of the size and savage character of this recent form from the report of Diest: 'In Delilerkoi I had a fight with a dozen savage shepherd-dogs which were about as large as my little horse and almost pulled me from my saddle.'

(Pumpelly, 1908)

A Kangal Dog plods along behind its sheep

It is interesting to see both how widespread and how uniform this breed of dog is throughout the region, even beyond the boundaries of Sivas province. A summer traveller taking the main road eastwards across Turkey (the ancient caravan route that runs through Ankara, Sivas and Erzurum towards Georgia and Iran) will pass countless flocks of sheep escorted by shepherd dogs. From Yozgat to Erzincan, a distance of around 450 km, almost every working dog will be a Kangal.

In this part of Turkey, where winter temperatures often plunge lower than –15 ºC, with deep snow, and summer temperatures may reach 40 ºC in the shade, only the hardiest animals survive and there is little natural prey for the wolves and jackals that inhabit this bleak landscape. Sheep and goats are therefore very much a target.

Physical traits

The physical characteristics of the Kangal Dog are ideally suited to the conditions in which it works as a protector of livestock. It is a large, powerfully built animal, heavy enough to take on predators but not molossoid (mastiff-like), being capable of covering the ground with great speed and agility. Yet for all its size and strength, this dog survives and indeed lives to quite an advanced age, about 12 years, on a meagre diet consisting almost entirely of cereal. Meat is a luxury eaten only occasionally by the villagers in rural Turkey, and it is only fed to dogs in the form of food scraps or carcass trimmings.

There is an element of camouflage in the appearance of this breed. To an onlooker watching the progress of a flock across the hillside, it may at first appear that there is no dog on guard, but closer inspection will probably reveal that what looked at first like a sheep, behind and slightly apart from the rest, is in fact a Kangal Dog plodding steadily along in the dust behind its charges.

When not on the move, the dog is quite likely to be standing or sitting quietly among the flock, which will be quite unperturbed by its proximity. With its characteristic pale fawn coat and black face, the dog is virtually undetectable from the local Akkaraman sheep, which are of similar size. On the alert, however, the

Kangal Dog signals its presence by carrying its long, slightly bushy tail high in a curl over its back. Under a good coating of Anatolian dust in the summer, the dog is also hard to spot against the sun-baked hillside where it will often station itself to keep watch over grazing animals in the valley. Stories abound of travellers who have been taken by surprise by a great dusty Kangal Dog suddenly hauling itself to its feet in front of them, apparently from nowhere, to bark a warning.

The functional double coat of the Kangal is perfectly adapted to the rigours of a working life spent out of doors in all conditions. It is short and close-lying, made up of a very dense soft undercoat covered by smooth, slightly longer and coarser hair that acts as a weatherproof jacket. The woolly under-layer provides insulation not only in the severe winters but against the fierce summer sun, and a complete twice-yearly moult modifies the thickness needed for the coming season. In winter, you can sink your fingers up to the second joint in this thick 'fleece'. The outer layer repels rain or snow, and mud, once dry, simply falls off the short, straight hair. The summer coat tends to be much less thick, and somewhat lighter in colour; a black or dark-coated dog would have a miserable time working in full sun with shade temperatures in the upper 30s ºC.

Kangal Dogs in the midst of their flock at sunset

The black mask of the Kangal Dog, another of the hallmarks of this breed, does more than lend expression to the face. The black shading around the eyes and on the muzzle helps to reduce glare from the sun, enhancing the dog's ability to distinguish objects at a distance. This has been tested in humans: in 2003 researchers at Yale University School of Medicine conducted a study of the effects of 'eye black' on athletes' visual acuity on the sports field. It was found that applying black greasepaint below the eyes assisted vision in conditions of bright sunlight and was in fact more effective than anti-glare stickers used by some sports players (Debroff and Pahk, 2003).

Black shading on the face reduces glare from bright sunlight

The eyes of the Kangal Dog are fairly small in relation to the size of the skull, with close-fitting eyelids. This again suits the windswept environment of the steppe, where large or prominent eyes would be constantly troubled by flying dust. The paws are fairly large and extremely strong with well-arched toes, thick, tough claws, and noticeable webbing between the toes. These dogs are very sure-footed, even at speed, in the stony and often unstable terrain.

Many shepherds set considerable store by the presence of hind dewclaws, and double dewclaws also commonly occur. However, no evidence has been found that these 'sixth toes' serve any practical purpose, since they have no muscular strength. Kangals are also great diggers, both in earth (to keep cool) and in snow (to keep warm), and they certainly have the right equipment for that task.

Chapter 4 Nature, adaptation, type

The development of breed type

It must be acknowledged that there are a great many Turkish shepherd dogs of no particular type, working effectively as guardians for sheep and goats. The Turkish name for any dog that does this work, whatever its shape or size, is *çoban köpeği*, 'shepherd dog', and type does vary, depending mainly on which part of Turkey the dog comes from. In the east and south-east of the country, in particular, there are still populations of nomadic herdsmen using dogs (*yürük* or *göcebe köpekleri*) which, although usually tall and strong, are very mixed in type and whose ancestors may have come from, for example, Syria, Georgia or Afghanistan.

The Kangal Dog, on the other hand, has emerged over time as a breed with particular attributes which, until comparatively recently, it has never been thought necessary to formalize into a written standard. Turkish people who work with animals—whether horses, production livestock, or dogs for hunting and protection—recognize the value of good type, steady temperament and predictable behaviour, and have maintained their own unofficial and mainly unwritten standards for centuries.

The earliest reliable account we have of shepherd dogs being bred selectively comes from the 17th-century writer and historian Evliya Çelebi. In his *Seyahatname* (*Book of Travels*, 1631–1670) he describes the ceremonial parades of the Janissaries, the elite Ottoman force, in which guarding dogs were displayed in full regalia by their keepers. The shepherds who formed part of this parade:

> … *lead in double or triple chains large dogs, the size of asses, and as fierce as lions, from the shores of Africa …. These dogs are covered with rich cloths, silver collars, and neck-rings, and a circle of iron points round the neck. Some of them are clad all in armour. They assail not only wolves, which enter the stables and folds, but would even attack dragons and rush into fire. The shepherds watch with great care the purity of the breed. They give for a leap [a mating] from such a dog one sheep and for a samsun or shepherd's dog of the true breed, five hundred sheep. These dogs are descended from the shepherd's dog which went into the cave in company with the Seven Sleepers. They chase the eagle in the air, the crocodile in the rivers, and are an excellent breed of well-trained dogs.*

The Seven Sleepers of Ephesus

There are many versions of this legend, which has long been popular in Christian tradition as well as appearing in the Koran. The following version is largely based on the poem by Johann Wolfgang von Goethe.

Seven young noblemen of Ephesus in the time of the Roman Emperor Decius (249–251 CE) refused to regard him as a god. They were accused of being Christians. Given time to recant, they fled to a nearby mountain to pray. There they took refuge in a cave and fell asleep.

> *By a shepherd led, they hastened*
> *To a cave was in the mountain,*
> *And they all went gliding in.*
> *And the shepherd's dog came after,*
> *Though they strove to drive him from them;*
> *Thrust himself towards his master,*
> *Licked their hands in dumb entreaty,*
> *That he may remain their fellow;*
> *And lay down with them to sleep.*

While the youths were sleeping in the cave, Decius sent soldiers to wall it up. The youths and the dog, Kitmir, were entombed in the cave.

> *So they lay and still beside them,*
> *Lay the dog in peaceful slumber,*
> *Never whimpering in its sleep.*

Decades passed and the youths eventually awoke in the time of Theodosius I (379–395 CE). According to one version, a farmer broke down the wall of the cave in order to use it as a cattle pen. Thinking they had slept for just a day, one of them went into the town of Ephesus for food. He was astonished to find buildings there with Christian crosses on. When he tried to buy bread with a coin from the reign of Decius, the people were amazed and suspected him of finding a treasure hoard. They called the local bishop to question the sleepers. After telling their story, they returned to the cave, and together with their faithful shepherd dog were again walled up and died praising God.

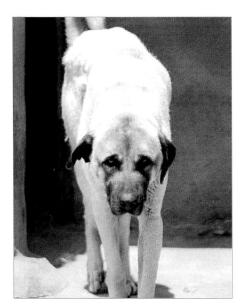

Kangal Dog in Ankara Zoo in 1985

Standards for the breed

Ankara Zoo has been exhibiting and breeding Kangal Dogs since the 1950s and the Turkish army has from time to time requisitioned dogs for guarding and for what is commonly referred to as 'man work' (although they have proved less successful in that capacity). The military's specification for a dog aged 1–3 years included the following points:

Weight:	54 kg minimum
Length:	79 cm
Height at shoulder:	76 cm
Face:	bright eyes; black markings around eyes, mouth, and forehead; black nose, triangular ears carried close to the head and pendant
Coat:	pale cream mixed with grey
Body:	powerful and muscular, back slightly longer than leg length, strong bone and wide chest; shoulders broad and muscular
Head:	size in proportion with body; foreface slightly more than one-third of total head length; lips black; square profile
Legs:	set well apart, straight with thick bones
Tail:	when relaxed, carried down with end slightly curled; when excited, carried over back in a strong curl
Movement:	when walking, head and neck in alignment.

Eventually, in 1997, the Turkish Standards Institute (Türk Standardlar Enstitüsü) included the Kangal Dog in its listing for purebred animals, under Standard No. 12172. The General Characteristics given in this standard were broadly in line with those of the Ankara Zoo specification, also describing the dog's tendency to be more active at night, its attachment to its owner and its flock, and its aversion to strangers and wild animals.

In the meantime, interest in Turkish dogs had grown among breeders of show dogs in Western Europe (see Chapter 7). A milestone in this trend was the collaboration between an American enthusiast, David Nelson; Cafer Tepeli, an academic from Selçuk University in Konya; Mehmet Ali Gül, manager of the municipal breeding centre in Kangal town; and Turhan Kangal, a senior member of a local landowning family that had adopted the name of the town during the social reforms of Atatürk. Together they agreed a breed standard for the Kangal Dog, built on the framework used by national kennel clubs for pedigree breeds. This document was signed and notarized in Turkey and later adopted by the United Kennel Club in the United States (1998) and the national kennel clubs of Australia, New Zealand and South Africa (1998, 1999, 2004).

It was not until 2005 that a more comprehensive Turkish breed standard for the Kangal Dog was published in the dog's own country. By this time various contradictory subjective accounts of the breed were in circulation. The aim of the study, conducted under the auspices of the Veterinary Faculty of Istanbul University and the Kangal Dog Breeding and Research Centre at Sivas Cumhuriyet University, was to:

> … *establish a written account of the breed characteristics of the Kangal Dog using standardized terminology, with a view to overcoming prevailing confusion over definitions and concepts and to providing a perspective for the breeding of Kangal Dogs in the future.*

(Özcan *et al.*, 2005)

As well as reviewing published papers and articles by individuals, the authors took advice from local breeders and farmers and examined examples of the breed in the field. A key player in this process was İlker Ünlü, a writer and researcher on Turkish dogs with an extensive knowledge of the international dog scene. He compiled and translated information from the numerous contributors to form a well-constructed, comprehensive document, following the format used by the world's major kennel clubs. The resulting standard was presented in July 2005 at an international symposium, held in the atmospheric surroundings of the 13th-century Alacahan caravanserai near Kangal town.

Breed Standard of the Kangal Dog

The Kangal dog is a large, strong livestock-guarding dog with an awe-inspiring stance and balanced proportions. The head is large; ears are medium-sized, black and pendant; a black mask covers nose and muzzle; coat colour varies from sand to pale grey; the short, dense, double coat and the tail carried in an open curl over the back forming a circle, when the dog is alert, are the typical characteristics of the breed.

Temperament and behaviour

The Kangal dog is a livestock-guarding dog. Instinctively it provides protection for sheep and goat flocks, guarding rather than herding them. It is courageous, fast and agile. It warns against danger and will pursue predators when necessary. It maintains a protective and balanced relationship with the animals in the herd. It prefers to act independently of the shepherd and to be free to protect the herd. It possesses strong instinctive working capabilities. It is full of love for and loyalty to its master. It is aloof to strangers; however, it does not display undue aggression.

Head and skull

The mesocephalic head is large but in good proportion with the body in general. The proportion of the foreface (from the stop to the tip of the nose) to the head length (from the occiput to the tip of the nose) is between 1:2.1 and 1:2.5 and foreface and forehead are parallel. Skull may show slightly raised occiput. While the head of the male dog resembles that of a lion, the head of the bitch is comparatively narrower and more elegant. The ears are set well apart and black. Characteristic black mask covers the nose and mouth.

Faults: *Dolichocephalic (narrow, long head) and brachycephalic (short-faced) head structure; extremely large head.*

Eyes

Eyes have an intelligent and trustworthy expression. In proportion to the head size, eyes are medium-sized, oval and deeply set. The eye rims are black. The colour of the eyes varies from honey yellow to brown. The white of the eye and the haw should not be visible.

Faults: *Large, round eye structure, drooping eyelids, light yellow eye colour.*

Nose and muzzle

The nose is prominent and blunt, with large nostrils. When the mouth is closed and observed from the side the nose is rectangular in profile. The muzzle is completely black including the lower jaw. There can be a black spot on the cheek. The structure of the jaws is strong. The teeth are well placed in the upper and lower jaws and upper and lower jaws close in a scissor bite. Black lips are pendulous enough to cover the lower jaw, but tight enough not to cause slobbering. The colour of the tongue is pink.

Faults: *Extremely pendulous lips; narrow, long nose.*

Ears

The ears are medium-sized, pendant and triangular in shape, rounded at the tips, placed at the outer edge of the head and set a little higher than the level of the eyes. The front edge of the ear can be measured to a spot near to the cheek and when pulled forward should have the length to overlap the eye. The colour of the ears is black, complementing the mask on the face.

Faults: *Straight ears; too short or too long ear size.*

Neck

The neck is slightly shorter than head length, thick, well muscled, slightly arched where it meets the head. Slight dewlap, especially seen in males.

Faults: *Too short or too long neck proportions; weak neck.*

Legs

The forelegs and hindlegs are large-boned, well muscled, strong and move in close co-ordination with the rest of the body. When observed from the front, the forelegs are parallel and straight to the ground; elbows are close to the chest. When observed from the back, hocks are parallel and straight to the ground. Hind legs are strong with moderate stifle angulation.

Faults: *Weak or poorly muscled legs; over- and under-angulation of the knee; hocks turning in or out.*

This working dog has strong feet with well-arched toes

A young Kangal with good conformation

The unique tail carriage of the Kangal Dog is a hallmark of the breed

Many Kangals, such as this mature male, have a grey rather than a fawn-coloured coat

Feet

The feet are large, strong and well arched. The nails are short and blunt. The colour of the nails can be white or black. The pads are well cushioned, dark in colour and firm. Hind dewclaws can be seen in some individuals. However, this is not a requirement.

Faults: *Narrow or splayed feet.*

Body structure

The body is well proportioned and strong. The back line flows gently from the shoulder, runs parallel to the ground and ends with a slightly arched tail end. The chest reaches down to the elbows; the ribs are substantial; abdomen is slightly drawn in. The loin is well muscled. Shoulder is strongly constructed and well muscled and at the same height as the rump. The parts of the body are firm, well muscled and without fat. The proportion of the shoulder height and body length is 1:1.2. This proportion gives the dog a slightly rectangular appearance. The proportion of chest width and chest depth is 1:1.5.

Faults: *Narrow and weak chest or cylinder-shaped body structure; extreme thinness.*

Tail

The tail reaches to the hock. The hair on the tail is denser than on the body. When relaxed, the tail is carried straight down to the hocks with the tip slightly curled upwards. When alert, the tail forms a single or double curl. The curled tail is carried in line with the spine, not falling to either side of the hip.

Faults: *Tail with too long hair (feathering) or with thin hair; insufficient curl; straight tail.*

Coat

The Kangal Dog is a short-coated breed. It has a double-layered coat structure formed of short and longer hair. The hair in the outer layer is longer and coarser. The undercoat is soft and dense. The hair on the neck and shoulder areas is longer than the hair on the other body parts. The hair on the face, head and ears is very short.

Faults: *A coat structure of too short or too long hair; wavy coat.*

Colour

Pale grey, pale yellow, pale brown coat colours can be seen. White colour markings can only be accepted on feet, up to the knees, and on chest. Characteristic black mask and ears. Other than these markings, solid overall coat colour is required.

Faults: *Lack of black mask; white markings on the chest and feet extending into main coat colour.*

Movement

The Kangal Dog has a calm and self-confident gait, suggesting inherent power and agility. The back remains straight when walking and at slow speed it can be observed from the side that fore and hind legs move parallel to each other (pacing). When trotting, diagonally opposite legs move in parallel. At the walk and the trot, the head and neck are held level with the line of the back. Strides are of moderate length, not short-stepping or over-reaching. As speed increases, so does the tendency to single-track.

Weight

50–70 kg in male dogs, 40–55 kg in bitches.

Height

70–85 cm in male dogs, 65–75 cm in bitches.

Disqualifications

• Unilateral or bilateral cryptorchidism
• Brown nose
• Albinism
• Harming stock (chasing, biting, killing); shy or fearful behaviour; failure to stay with the flock; extreme and uncontrolled aggression
• Lack of black mask; white markings on face
• Blue, green, black eye colour
• Undershot or overshot jaw
• Tail not curled over back when alert
• Colour other than the stated standard coat colours; multicolour or striped coat colour; white markings on any part of the coat other than below knees and chest.

At the walk and trot the head and neck are held level with the line of the back

Even at a few months old, this puppy displays the classic Kangal gait

This standard was published in the proceedings of the 2nd International Kangal Dog Symposium (Ograk (ed.), 2005)

Kangals at work

Flocks in Turkey are reared extensively, over wide stretches of scrubby grassland that changes with the seasons in quality and availability.

When the snows in the Sivas area clear in March and April, the rivers are full and grazing becomes abundant, consisting of tough grasses and aromatic herbs, mainly bluegrass and wheatgrass, thymes and artemisia (Karagöz, 2001/2006). At this time of year the sheep are escorted by the shepherd and his dogs from the precincts of the village to pastures a few kilometres away and they return at dusk.

As the summer approaches, there is a need to travel further to find good grazing, up on to the higher slopes of the steep hillsides and mountains. This can involve long journeys, and so the time-honoured system of transhumance has become part of the seasonal pattern of village life in the region. The sheep, and the dogs that guard them, live on the high pastures, the *yaylalar*, throughout the summer, and some of the villagers accompany them, continuing to milk the sheep and make cheese and yoghurt in the temporary shelters they build there.

When the weather closes in again, the community is reunited in the village and the animals return to graze, first on the stubble of the harvested fields around the settlements and then on stored fodder while they are housed under cover during the harshest months. In the severe winters, roads are impassable and many villages in the Sivas area are completely cut off by deep snow. Livestock are kept in low, mud brick-built barns and fodder is stored to quite a depth on the flat rooftops of these barns and of the houses, adding welcome insulation for the comfort of the animals and the families living below. In these winter months the Kangal Dogs will still be on guard around the villages, because wolves regularly come close to scavenge. The dogs may live in the barn with the livestock or dig themselves a burrow next to their master's house.

A clever Kangal might tuck itself up for the night among the fodder on the roof, with only its black face peeping out as it keeps watch. If the dogs sense the presence of a wolf they bark a warning and are released by the villagers to chase it away.

Working behaviour

Wherever the flocks are grazing away from the village, Kangal Dogs will generally work in pairs, or teams for a larger flock, taking up positions around the sheep and changing shift from time to time. They do not waste energy by running around needlessly and in the daytime are content to lie still and quiet. A Kangal on duty out on the mountainside will usually station itself on a high vantage-point

A sheltered spot, dug out beside his master's house

Signalling the approach of strangers while sheep graze in safety

overlooking its flock and simply watch and listen. In the full heat of the day the dog will dig itself a cool hollow in the ground and settle into it, becoming almost invisible to anyone approaching.

The night watch, however, is a different matter, for it is then that the dogs actively patrol along a wide perimeter, sounding their presence from time to time as they go.

Encounters with danger

The behaviour of the Kangal Dog when its suspicions are aroused is fascinating to watch. First of all it will stand full-square, tail curled high over its back, and ears up listening. Then there will be a quiet 'wuff', just enough to signal to the sheep that something is up, followed by the sharp bark that is the signal to the other dogs and the shepherd to get into position.

The sheep, which have learned to trust the dog, will bunch together and—far from moving away, as would a flock used to being driven by a herding dog—gather towards their protector. The Kangal's first instinct is to place itself between the perceived source of danger and its sheep or master; it will trot back and forth across the line of approach, gradually coming closer to them. (This is a very powerful instinct and one that can be observed in Kangal Dogs that have never seen active service but live in a domestic setting in other countries: faced with a stranger, the dog will stand across its owner's path until assured that it is safe to allow the unfamiliar person to approach.)

With the sheep safely behind it, and back-up alerted, the Kangal can then go out to confront the intruder and the bark becomes a full-throated roar, an unmistakable threat. Working as a team, one dog may go after a wolf while another stays to protect the flock, because they understand that the first wolf could be a decoy and others may be lurking. Pursuit of the wolf has been known to continue for days over many kilometres, sometimes with the dog ending up in another village so that the owners have to be called to retrieve it. Good Kangal Dogs are known by name, and by their owner's name, throughout the neighbourhood.

Collars for working Kangals

Working Kangal Dogs in Turkey, like their counterparts in other countries in the Near East and Central Asia, customarily wear spiked metal collars to protect the throat in an attack by wolves or other predators. As soon as the young dog begins its working life the shepherd will provide it with an iron collar fitted with very sharp, and sometimes quite long, spikes. Here are three designs, and one modelled by a Kangal.

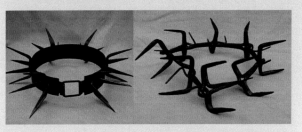

Above left, a solid metal band with spikes welded to it; above right, articulated open sections bent into spikes; below left, articulated oval plates with extensions bent into spikes

Usually the dog needs to do no more than chase off the interloper, but a hungry, desperate or foolhardy wolf may stand its ground, in which case the dog will run forward at great speed and, using its substantial forehand weight, hurl a shoulder against the wolf to knock it to the ground. It will then attack the throat and the hindlegs.

Villages and local markets sometimes display the skin of an unlucky wolf as a trophy or for sale, and shepherds may keep a piece of wolf skin to tease Kangal puppies as they grow into the job of their elders.

Learning the job

It is universally accepted among people who use Kangals to protect livestock that the unique skills these dogs possess are not learned by training at the hands of their owners or handlers. They learn from each other. A steady, experienced Kangal is the shepherd's most valuable asset, not only because he knows it will be a trustworthy guardian for his stock, but because the job of training the new generation will largely be done by that dog—or, just as often, that bitch. A novice dog will be sent out to work in the company of an older one and will learn its technique by experience; in the process, the newcomer will also learn where it stands in the hierarchy of dogs.

In and around the villages in Turkey, dogs, sheep and goats form a community in which puppies grow up to understand how they must behave and what liberties they can get away with, or not. Sooner or later someone will correct them; if not an older Kangal, then maybe a butt from a cantankerous old ewe or goat will teach them their manners if they start to tease the young stock.

In more Western countries, farmers and researchers have made quite a study of methods of 'bonding' livestock-guarding dogs to sheep. With fewer dogs available and a quite different farming environment, it is simply not possible to leave things to chance, so interaction has to be monitored and unruly juvenile behaviour controlled by the farmer to some extent.

New pups are usually housed alongside stock, then penned with one or two sheep or goats (with a puppy-sized retreat to escape to), and later gradually introduced to the rest of the flock under supervision as they grow bigger. It is important not to expect too much of a new Kangal youngster: it may well take two years for a young dog to become reliable with stock, and there are often setbacks along the way, so patience is needed. Here too, the best training aid is the older, experienced Kangal, and it is worth remembering that, given suitable care and conditions, this breed can live to the age of 12 years or more. In its lifetime a good Kangal can train many generations of reliable guardians.

İnci Willard farms Katahdin sheep in Pennsylvania and keeps Kangals to protect them: Lokum, age 4, Tomas, imported from Turkey and now probably about 10 years old, and their two pups Çelik (male) and Benek (female), 12 months old. İnci writes:

Kangal pups in California get to know their goats

> *We have lots of coyotes around here. Most neighbours with sheep and goats get hit regularly, even with their donkeys and llamas on guard, but we no longer get them anywhere near us. […]*
>
> *We walk sheep back to home base through an old logging path from the pasture about a mile away. The lead dog is always our matriarch, Lokum. Tomas always trails the sheep, for he likes to mark the standing trees as we go along, and the pups disappear into the midst of the flock. If Lokum stops, the sheep come to a standstill, even with the Border Collie driving them from behind. If Lokum starts growling, Benek immediately peels off and takes position by her side. If Benek starts barking, Lokum first of all backs into the sheep and then she'll get on the outside of the circle to check them. The moment Benek begins to charge towards whatever is disturbing her, brother Celik peels off to back her. Old Tomas looks bored, most probably thinking 'silly pups'.*
>
> *Both Lokum and Tomas accompany the sheep to the hay field for early winter grazing where there is no fencing; I can safely leave them there overnight and take their food to them in the morning. I have not yet taken the youngsters out there, as they have just turned a year old, but knowing how they have formed a tight pack, I doubt that they will try to follow me home once they understand that 'this is where we eat now'.*

In its lifetime a good Kangal can train many generations of reliable guardians

For anyone wishing to explore the practical aspects of raising dogs with livestock, books such as *Livestock Guardians* (Dohner, 2007) and *Livestock Protection Dogs – Selection, care and training* (Dawydiak and Sims, 2004) give very helpful guidance.

The first meeting between 12-week pups and sheep on the Lamberts' farm in California

On İnci Willard's farm, a 4-week Kangal (note the dark grey puppy coat) investigates the sheep's grain feeder, supervised by its mother

A spring day on the *yayla*

*A working day in Doymuş hamlet, near Kangal,
described by one of the authors*

The *yayla* hamlet of Doymuş lies about 10 km from Havuz. Here, three related families spend May to December grazing two flocks on the uplands. We joined farmer Salim Dikçal, his two young sons, and his elderly father, Asım Bey, as they set out for the long day grazing their flock on the *yayla*.

It is 7 o'clock on a warm, sunny morning in May. Four Kangal Dogs lie around the grassy space between the three houses and barns. They have already had their only meal of the day, a bowl of *yal,* to sustain them for the day ahead. Suddenly a donkey emerges from a barn, followed by a bleating flock of about 150 sheep. Simultaneously another barn door is opened to release a similar-sized flock of lambs, who rush towards the adult flock searching frantically for their mothers for their morning milk. The air is filled with deafening bleating from both flocks as this desperate search and feeding frenzy continues.

Gradually the flock moves slowly away towards the hillsides, the sheep nibbling the grass and suckling their lambs as they go. The younger lambs are caught and taken back to their barn, while the older ones stay with the adult flock. As we climb slowly up the hillside we see three of the dogs disappearing behind the barn. Dogless, the flock spreads out across the slopes and the bleating abates as sheep and lambs start to graze the low-growing pads of succulent plants.

We reach the plateau, the sun beating down relentlessly. A donkey arrives, ridden by a young man from one of the other families of the hamlet. The dogs we saw are with him, for he is their owner. He throws them bits of his breakfast bread as he moves off to his own flock up ahead. Salim Bey tells us that the dogs will only go with the shepherd if they like him. Otherwise they stay in the village. He also explains the functions of the donkey. Basically it is for carrying the water and food needed for the day out on the *yayla*, as well as the *kepenek*, the shepherd's felt cape. Even in this hot weather, the donkey carries a *kepenek*. The donkey also comes in useful for taking a sick animal back to the village and it provides transport for tired shepherds at the end of the day.

The dogs hang about behind the flock as it moves slowly across the treeless plateau, and they lie down at every opportunity. They appear uninterested in their surroundings but should there be a wolf in the vicinity, Salim Bey tells us, they will sense it and give chase. This apparently happens several times a year.

The day heats up. We take our leave. Two hours has been as much as we can take, but the flock, dogs, donkey and shepherds will spend the rest of the day wandering the uplands under the burning sun.

At noon the flock will be gathered together. The sheep will settle down to chew the cud, the shepherds will sit down to have their lunch and the dogs will lie down to rest. Then they will spend the afternoon slowly moving back to the hamlet, arriving at about 7 o'clock in the evening, when another feeding frenzy occurs as the young lambs held in the barn during the day seek their mothers' milk.

With the flocks back in the barn for the night, the shepherds can relax at home. The dogs lie about the yard, dozing but alert as darkness falls. It's the end of another long hot day on the *yayla*.

Life in Kangal country

The social and economic environment in which the Kangal Dog lives and works today has an important bearing on its chances of survival into the future in its home territory and elsewhere.

The Kangal has developed over the centuries to fill a specific need as a working dog, which is to guard the flocks of the central Anatolian steppes, particularly the flocks of the Kangal Akkaraman breed of sheep of the Sivas-Kangal region. This need is now changing and with it the role of the Kangal Dog.

Village society

Scattered thinly across the bare landscape of the Sivas-Kangal region are farming villages and hamlets, many small and isolated. Some are cut off from the outside world by heavy snowfalls in the winter months. The people of these villages live a simple existence, relatively unchanged for centuries. Although modern technology has arrived in the form of electricity, tractors and television, daily life tends to follow age-old patterns, dictated by the weather and seasons. Life is slower, there is always time to sit and chat, to welcome visitors, offering tea, warm milk or *ayran* (a yoghurt drink) and homemade bread. Visiting a village is like going back in time.

People are aware of the history of their villages and the origins of their families. Some villages are said to have been established relatively recently, within the last 200 to 300 years, such as Esenyurt near Sivas, originally a mainly Armenian village. The majority, however, are said to be over 500 years old and most people trace their origins back to Central Asia as part of the gradual movement westwards of Turkic tribes over the centuries.

Esenyurt village near Sivas: Ömer and Özgür in their school uniform with Şirin, the Kangal bitch belonging to their grandparents, Ömer and Fatma Gülsever

Three generations of the Kadırtaş family. The grandfather (seated) arrived in Maltepe as a baby in 1923 after a sea journey from Salonika and travelling over the mountains from Samsun in a cart

Religion

As with the general population of Turkey, the vast majority of villagers follow a Moslem way of life. Most Turkish Moslems are Sunnis, but there is also a substantial minority, 20 million out of a population of approximately 70 million, who are Alevis. The Alevi sect of Turkey is said to conserve true Anatolian folk culture. Their religious rituals differ markedly from those of the mainstream Sunnis in Turkey. Alevis use the Turkish or Kurdish language in their rituals, rather than Arabic. They do not worship in mosques; instead they meet in an assembly house called a *cemevi*. Their prayer rituals involve singing and dancing. Men and women are regarded as equals and pray side by side. Within Turkish society Alevis are generally regarded as liberal in outlook and lifestyle. They have traditionally been strong supporters of the secularist reforms of Kemal Atatürk. As a heterodox sect, they have suffered ridicule and oppression in the past and there have been a number of pogroms. Even as recently as 1993, an arson attack by a mob on the Madımak Hotel in the city of Sivas caused the deaths of 37 people attending an Alevi cultural festival.

In the Kangal district there is a tendency for villages to be fairly homogeneous in terms of religion: there are Sunni villages, distinguished by the presence of a mosque, often with its distinctive minaret; and there are Alevi villages, which do not have a mosque. There are also some mixed villages. The extensive Alevi presence in the Sivas-Kangal area is an important factor in the social fabric of the district.

Moslem attitudes towards dogs

According to the Koran, Moslems are required to treat all living creatures with compassion and should not abuse them. Although dogs are generally considered unclean, Moslems are expected to treat them with respect. Thus in Turkey most people will not take a dog into their house but they will keep a dog in the garden or put out food in the street for stray animals. The *hadith*s, accounts of the sayings and deeds of the Prophet Mohammed, also mention the treatment of animals. People are to be consigned to hell for maltreating animals, or rewarded with a place in paradise for kindness towards them. One *hadith* (Bukhari: Volume 4, Book 54, No. 538) describes how a 'sinful person' possibly a prostitute, seeing a thirsty dog hanging about near a well, fills a shoe with water and gives it to the dog. This person is rewarded with God's forgiveness.

However, it is one thing to take care of the bodily needs of a dog; it is another to show friendliness towards it, to pat it, to talk to it. Some practising Moslems in Turkey will avoid touching a dog or even having it touch their clothing, in the belief that this contact will nullify their purity before they carry out their ritual prayers. Others will not be concerned at all. In many districts of Istanbul, for example, there are street dogs that are regarded as neighbourhood pets. Besides naming them and feeding them, people can be seen patting and playing with them. In the villages shepherds often show great fondness for their dogs, stroking and talking to them, their only companions in the loneliness of the steppe. Village women and children, too, handle and play with the family's dogs, bringing food and watching over puppies.

Cruelty to animals is a universal problem, not necessarily a cultural or religious one. Judging by material on the internet, Turkey seems to have a bad reputation for its treatment of animals. Yet one of the authors of this book has personally seen many instances of care and kindness towards animals during more than 30 years in Turkey—for example, the sight of a municipal bus driver on the busy Bosphorus main road, stopping his bus to allow a cat and a procession of kittens to cross the road. It is true that many children are brought up to fear dogs, which is understandable in a country where rabies is endemic and stray dogs are common. However, it is also true that cruelty to all animals is condemned by Moslem teaching, and kindness is believed to be rewarded.

Preparing yal and looking after puppies in the village

Höbek

Höbek village (pop. 254) lies just off the road between Kangal and Divriği. The *muhtar*, Mustafa Karadeniz, explains that the village is about 700 years old and that his family has lived there throughout that time, the population originally having migrated from Central Asia via Elazığ. This is an Alevi village, although Armenians also lived here in the past. Mustafa Bey emphasizes that in an Alevi village all kinds of people live peacefully together.

Mustafa Bey is an important landowner in Höbek. He has a herd of cows, rather than sheep, and has seven Kangal Dogs to guard them against wild boar and wolves, which prey on the calves. He talks of the faithfulness of Kangals, telling how he once left his coat behind in a cornfield. One of his Kangals went missing for 3 days. Then someone told him that his dog had been seen out in the fields, where it had been guarding Mustafa Bey's coat ever since he left it there!

Mustafa Bey is clearly fond of his dogs. He does not crop their ears. He finds the bitches more alert, friendlier with people, and better workers than his male dogs, which are more aggressive. When giving away puppies he always checks out prospective owners. One person requested a puppy and asked for it to be put on the bus to him in Istanbul. Mustafa Bey refused this request. 'I would not send a puppy alone,' he says. 'If someone wants puppies they must come here to me for them.'

Turhan Kangal

Turhan Kangal is a well-known figure in Kangal district. He traces his family ancestry back to the Türkmen nomads who came to Anatolia in the 14th century. His branch of the family settled in this district and was given the lordship of the area, comprising 30–40 villages, by one Abdurrahman Paşa. Thus they became the Kangal *ağalar* (lords). In 1934, as part of Atatürk's reform programme, all Turkish families were required to choose surnames and Turhan Bey's family naturally chose the surname Kangal. The family have given away some of their villages, such as the village of Armağan, which means 'gift'.

In the past the family were important livestock owners and breeders of horses. Turhan Bey used to have a great many dogs working with his flocks, but now that he no longer keeps sheep he has no dogs either. As he puts it, 'The dog without the sheep is nothing.' He says that the name Kangal has been used for this breed of dog at least since his great-great-grandfather's time.

The Kadi and 'Karabaş'

Once upon a time there was a shepherd who had a beautiful dog named Karabaş. Karabaş was such a good sheep dog! No matter whether the shepherd was present or not, he would protect the flock from all kinds of danger. He would never allow wolves to get near the sheep. If a wolf even approached the flock, he would catch it and strangle it. He was such a strong dog!

One day, however, Karabaş became ill, and soon after that he died. The shepherd loved him so much that he gave Karabaş a fine funeral, just as if he had been a human being. He had him washed and wrapped in a white linen shroud, and then he had him buried in a Moslem cemetery. As there are busybodies all over the world, so there was one in this village too. He went to the kadi [a *kadı* is a judge of Islamic law] and complained that the shepherd had held a Moslem funeral for his dog and that he had buried him in a grave among those of the faithful. 'It is a sacrilegious act,' said this busybody, 'and I demand that he be punished.'

The shepherd was summoned to court and the kadi asked him, 'How is it that you give an unclean creature a Moslem burial and place him in a grave among the faithful? Don't you know that this is a blasphemous thing to do?'

In his own defence the shepherd said, 'Efendi, so great was the service of this dog to me that during his life I presented him with thirty sheep as a token of my appreciation. When the dog was about to die, he said to me, "When I am dead, kill ten of my sheep and spend the money from them on my funeral expenses; kill ten more and give the money they bring to the poor."'

'That makes twenty sheep,' said the kadi. 'What about the rest?'

'Well,' said the shepherd, 'he placed the remaining ten at the disposal of the kadi of this area and said that he should do whatever he thinks appropriate with them.'

Very pleased with this arrangement, the kadi inquired, 'What was the name of the deceased?' When the shepherd told him it was Karabaş, the kadi opened his hands toward heaven and addressing all those present, he said, 'Join me, O faithful, in a prayer for the soul of Karabaş.'

(Walker and Uysal, 1966)

The village scene

Traditional villages in the central Anatolian region of Turkey consist of flat-roofed, often whitewashed houses built from mud bricks and rendered. The village house shown here, belonging to the Kaya family, has just received a smart new adobe render, which is drying in the summer sunshine. The grass roof is characteristic of this style of house.

Cool in summer and warm in winter, these houses are sometimes built into the hillside and the family may grow cucumbers, tomatoes and melons on the sun-baked rooftop. To visitors walking through a hillside village, it may come as a surprise to discover that they are walking on the grassy roof of someone's house; the only telltale sign of what is underfoot may be a small white chimney-stack protruding from the ground.

The interior of the village house is immaculate, its white walls decorated with hangings and family pictures and the floors covered in colourful carpets and kilims woven to the local design. Sofas and cushions, upholstered with beautiful embroidery, fold out to make extra beds for guests.

Nothing goes to waste in the village. Animal dung is a valuable resource: when the barns are cleared, it is dried and made into briquettes for fuel. These are stored in neatly built stacks around the village throughout the summer season

A visit to Hocabey village

The Türkseven family. The grandfather pictured here spoke fluent German, having worked for many years in German coalmines

Home-baked Turkish bread is a treat that comes in many shapes and sizes

The authors describe their meeting with some of the people of Hocabeyköy.
This village lies only 15 km from the modern city of Sivas, but it lives in another age.

The road winds up through a rocky gorge and emerges into a wide green valley. Fields of young wheat and barley carpet the valley floor. In the distance a group of trees borders a stream. We approach a brown and white village, each mud-rendered house surrounded by high white stone walls.

We enter a wide grassy terrace. Two old men are sitting on a wall enjoying the late afternoon sun. We stop the car and they move slowly towards us. Can they tell us the way to the *muhtar*'s house? A tall young girl playing nearby pipes up, 'He's my uncle. I can show you.' But one of the old men climbs into the front seat and we set off again, winding through the dusty lanes until we reach a big two-storeyed house. In the back yard two young women are washing large copper pans in a trough of running water.

People gather, chairs are produced, tea is offered, and we settle down for a chat. The people believe that their village is over 600 years old. There used to be 100 households but now there are only 35, most of the inhabitants having migrated to Germany.

The village has 550 sheep, down from more than 1000 ten years ago. There are twelve dogs, most of which are out on the surrounding hills with their sheep, usually working five to a flock (two female and three male). Apart from wolves one of their problems is the aggressive wild boar, which inhabit the woods along the stream. The dogs are effective in killing the boar but at a terrible cost, for the tusks can inflict severe injuries.

We ask the villagers to tell us what they look for in a good Kangal Dog and they describe a dog with a big head, thick neck, broad chest, black face and pale body, dewclaws, and a very curly tail held over the back. But they admit that they do not have such good dogs in their own village now.

Before we leave we are invited to see bread being baked in the house. We enter a wide, dark, earthen-floored space on the ground floor. At one side is a low platform in front of a large wood-burning clay oven in which the women of the household are baking flat round loaves. After taking family photos and shaking hands all round, we reluctantly depart for Sivas and the 21st century.

Karşıyaka *mahallesi* (district)

May is shearing time in Karşıyaka *mahallesi*, near Kangal. As Mustafa Ceylan and his family expertly clipped their Akkaraman sheep, he explained that the wool from these sheep was for a special purpose: it was to be made into the mattress of a new wedding bed. Sheep's wool is also used in Turkey to fill traditional handmade quilts, many of them true works of art, covered in beautiful designs and embroidery.

Mustafa Bey retired to the farm after working in the military clothing business. However, sheep farming had recently become more difficult since the provincial government had embarked on its tree-planting scheme, because sheep were not allowed to graze on forestry land.

He had bought his Kangal Dog, in exchange for a load of hay, from a local village known to have good examples of the breed. Wolves were a regular threat to his sheep. He told of a dog he once had that was so reliable that it would take the flock to pasture and bring it safely home without any kind of supervision. From their farmhouse, he and his wife could watch the flock moving around the distant hillsides supervised by their Kangal guardian. Sadly, one day the dog was stolen; he had no doubt that it was because of its reputation as a good shepherd dog.

The Kangal Akkaraman sheep

The Kangal breed of the White Karaman (Akkaraman) fat-tailed sheep is raised in the Sivas and Malatya provinces of Turkey. Fat-tailed sheep in general are hardy and adaptable, able to withstand the harsh, dry climates of the Near and Middle East and Central Asia. They have been bred for the fat stored in the tail, which can weigh up to 6 kg and is an important ingredient in traditional cuisine in these regions.

The Kangal Akkaraman sheep is a particularly large breed, almost 70 cm high at the withers. It is white with a short, fine inner coat and longer, coarse outer coat. Like the Kangal Dog, it has a black muzzle and black around the eyes. It is a truly multipurpose breed, farmed for its meat, milk and wool.

At the Kangal Festival proud owners show off their dogs in the parade

Kangal pups accompany their mothers to the event

Social life

Social life in Kangal town and the villages in the area is generally limited to family events and annual religious celebrations, such as Ramazan Bayram at the end of the month of fasting, and Kurban Bayram when sheep and other animals are sacrificed in memory of Abraham and Isaac. Alevis also celebrate a spring holiday called Nevruz. Occasionally visiting theatrical groups or performers will appear in the Kangal wedding hall. But the most exciting event on the social and cultural calendar of the district is the Kangal Festival.

The Kangal Festival

The festival takes place every year for three days (Friday, Saturday, Sunday), usually in the second week of July, in the town of Kangal and in the surrounding district. Events at the festival include Turkish traditional and popular music concerts, dinners, and visits to chosen villages, where guests are entertained with folk music and dancing. The Turkish love of hospitality is very much in evidence in the villages, where often large numbers of guests are welcomed and entertained. Traditional dishes are served, such as pilav and sweet puddings made from cereal and fruit.

But the highlight of the festival is the Kangal Dog contest. This is held at the Kangal Dog Breeding Centre on the outskirts of the town and usually takes up most of the Saturday of the festival weekend. The dogs and their owners come from the Sivas-Kangal area and also from other parts of Turkey, over 200 dogs taking part in recent years.

In the arena at the Kangal Festival a troupe of schoolgirls perform folk dances

The dogs are provided with a waiting area in the grassy grounds of the centre. Those registered to take part in the final judging in the ring are provided with a red ribbon to wear, and a ring number. The dogs wait patiently, almost all of them quite happy to be patted and admired by festival visitors. It is clear that the dogs are loved and cared for by their owners and most feel at ease with people, even strangers.

They are generally shown in two main classes, *Bekci* (factory/domestic guards) and *Sürü* (flock guards), and are then sub-categorized by age.

Waiting to go into the ring

One by one the finalists are led before a panel of judges, which includes vets from the area and from Cumhuriyet University. This contest generates great interest among the owners and spectators. The owners are extremely proud of their dogs, each believing his dog is the best, and the announcement of results can lead to heated exchanges. Medals are presented to the winning dogs in each class.

In conjunction with the festival, symposiums on the Kangal Dog are occasionally held. At the 7th International Kangal Festival in 2005 a one-day symposium took place at the unusual venue of the Alacahan caravanserai. In the cavernous interior lit by shafts of natural light from roof vents, papers were presented by academics from several Turkish universities, as well as speakers from the USA, Britain and Slovakia. It was on this occasion that the Turkish breed standard for the Kangal Dog (described in Chapter 4) was presented. Other topics included the genetics, care and breeding of Kangals and their use in wild carnivore conservation.

On show at the Kangal Festival

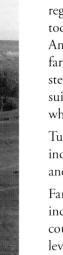

The local economy

For thousands of years the economy of the Sivas-Kangal region has depended on farming and this continues today. Its geographical location, in the centre of the Anatolian Plateau, has always determined the type of farming carried out. The combination of wide rolling steppe and continental climatic conditions provides a suitable environment for growing cereals, particularly wheat and barley, and for rearing sheep.

Turkey's wool production is for the domestic textiles industry and, importantly, for its famous carpets and kilims.

Farming methods are still largely traditional and farm incomes are very low compared with other European countries, but efforts are being made to raise production levels closer to standards in the European Union. One initiative, for example, is the Sheep Husbandry Project jointly funded by the EU and the Turkish government. This project involves farmers in a series of four weekly sessions taught by university lecturers, agricultural engineers and veterinarians. Farmers from several villages gather in the meeting room of a conveniently located village to attend the lectures and discussions, at the end of which they are tested and receive a certificate. In 2007 about 100 farmers took part in this programme.

Kangal Balıklı Kaplıca

The fish spa is probably unique in the world, in that the treatment it offers is based on small fish, which live in the warm water of thermal springs. Sufferers of psoriasis soak in the thermal pools containing two types of fish, both members of the Cyprinidae family, which are adapted to living in the 35 °C water. The 'striker' fish nibbles away the diseased flesh and the 'licker' fish cleans the wound. It is claimed that by following this treatment for 21 days, spending 8 hours a day in the pool, a sufferer has a 98 per cent chance of recovery, without using any kind of drugs or ointments.

Apart from farming, two other contributions to the economy of the Kangal district are worth mentioning, health tourism at the Balıklı Kaplıca 'doctor fish spa', and the coal-fired power station with its related lignite coal mining operation.

Situated 14 km from Kangal town, the fish spa has a 300-bed hotel, conference centre and restaurant. This and the treatment facilities provide some employment opportunities for local people.

The Sivas region is rich in minerals of many kinds, some quite rare, and mining is an important activity in the province. Coal is mined at Kangal by the Demir Export Company which, together with the Kangal Thermal Power Station which it supplies, is the biggest non-agricultural employer in the district.

The local landscape has undergone a number of changes in recent years as various civil engineering projects have been undertaken in the area. Turkey is an important 'energy bridge' between Central Asia and western Europe and major pipelines run across Sivas province. Some carry natural gas and one, the huge Baku–Tblisi–Ceyhan (BTC) pipeline, carries crude oil from Azerbaijan, on the Caspian Sea, to the Mediterranean coast at Ceyhan in southern Turkey.

Water management projects are also underway in Sivas, involving the construction of dams and irrigation systems. Despite schemes to compensate local communities, the environmental and social impact of these developments has been substantial and often less than sympathetic to the needs and lifestyle of villagers.

Rural exodus and decline in sheep rearing

With limited work opportunities in this spartan environment, unless the rural economy is improved it is inevitable that people will continue to leave the countryside to find work in urban areas, such as the city of Sivas and further afield in Ankara, Istanbul or even other countries. The number of households (*haneler*) in each village in the Kangal area visited by the authors has declined markedly over the last two decades. Some examples illustrate the trend. In Deliktaş village 20 years ago there were 350 households, in 2007 only 70 households. In Hüyüklüyurt in the same period households had declined from 100 to 40.

In this socio-economic situation the future of the Kangal Dog is in jeopardy. As an integral part of the agricultural economy of the Sivas-Kangal area, any change in that economy will have a direct effect on the Kangal Dog, the most obvious threat being the decline in sheep husbandry. In village after village the story was the same: there were fewer flocks than in previous years. Here Kangals are kept, not as pets, but as working dogs, so if the number of flocks declines, so does the need for dogs to guard them. Like the sheep, Kangal Dogs are gradually disappearing from the countryside.

A shepherd at work in Kangal district

Yelliceköyü

Yelliceköyü lies on a hillside, 40 km from Kangal on the road to Divriği. This is an Alevi village comprising 40–50 households in winter and more than 100 in summer, when villagers return from the cities. Historically, the population came from Horusan in Iran, and the village land was given by the *ağa* (lord) of Kangal.

According to Veli Sönmez, the village *muhtar*, in 2007 the village had 500–600 sheep in four small flocks guarded by about 10 dogs. The *muhtar* himself had given up sheep rearing 4 years previously as being uneconomic, citing the cost of paying a shepherd and supplying fodder when the sheep spend 5 months of the year indoors. He also mentioned that the demand for fleeces had declined with the increased use of synthetics. His income now depended on crops of wheat and barley. The family also made cheese from cow's milk.

Hüyüklüyurt

This village takes its name from the nearby Hittite mound (*hüyük/höyük*), used nowadays as the village cemetery. Today's inhabitants moved here from Deliktaş 150–200 years ago. Although the number of households has declined from 100, some 20 years ago, to 40 today (35 in winter), during the last 5 years migration has halted. *Muhtar* Sabahattin Vural puts this down to state support. In addition, the village is less isolated today as improved transport enables villagers to visit the city easily, for shopping, medical treatment and so on. Flocks had declined in the past, but Vural Bey was now gradually increasing his flock size by 25 sheep per year.

Beyyurdu village – back to the land?

Although the current trend is for people to leave the countryside and head for the cities, one young woman is moving back to the land, although only up to a point.

Feride Karasu

Feride Karasu grew up in the city of Sivas and runs a café there. She had never visited her family's land near Kangal until the death of her parents, when she inherited 360 *dönum* (90 acres) in the hamlet of Beyyurdu. Now she is having a house built there and plans to plant barley and wheat on the land and to keep bees. However, like the other landowners of Beyyurdu, she will only live in the hamlet during the summer, thus keeping a foot in both worlds.

The reasons given for this by the flock owners are various. The cost of paying a shepherd is one reason; it is difficult for the villagers to compete with the salaries offered to workers in the city. The cost of winter fodder is also cited. In some areas forestry planting has reduced the flocks as grazing areas are more restricted and farmers are fined if their stock damage the young trees. The advent of tractors in the villages has made possible the cultivation of land that previously could only be used for grazing by sheep and goats. Irrigation has also increased crop growing at the expense of animal husbandry.

An interesting local initiative has been proposed to reduce the rural exodus and at the same time to protect the two local breeds, the Kangal sheep and the Kangal Dog, both of which are seen as endangered by rural decline in the region. The overall aim is to encourage local people to stay in the area by developing alternative income sources and by providing better living standards. This would be achieved by supporting the production of sheep and dogs in their natural environment and by developing agro-tourism, an activity that would involve hosting tourists in the villages. Living conditions in the countryside would be improved in order to make this possible. Sponsorship for this project has been sought from European Union funds aimed at protecting traditional cultures in Europe, as Turkey moves towards attaining EU standards.

Hopes for the future

Public awareness of the Kangal Dog and pride in the breed are increasing in Turkey, fuelled by TV documentaries, books and newspaper articles, and by the Kangal Festival. Recognition of the dog's value as a national resource should grow as a result. Although the number of flocks and their attendant dogs in the Sivas-Kangal area have declined in recent years, there are now small signs that the tide may be turning. Rural development projects, in progress and in the pipeline, aim to make village life more attractive, thus stemming migration to the cities. Turkey's planned accession to the European Union is driving attempts to improve stock yields and raise standards generally in rural areas. If the socio-economic environment in the region improves, so should the future prospects of the Kangal Dog in its homeland.

A farmer of the future? Young Yasin Dikçal helps his family with their flock at the summer pastures of Doymuş hamlet. Yasin has been given a lamb of his own to raise. When the mature sheep is sold Yasin plans to buy a bicycle with the proceeds

Kangals abroad

Kangals have become established as working dogs in the USA, Australia, New Zealand and southern Africa, where they are able to function in much the same role as they have in their homeland.

After some initial false starts in successfully bonding the dogs to their flocks, farmers have become experienced in the use of livestock guardians and have made significant reductions in losses of sheep and goats to coyotes, dingoes, feral dogs and rustlers.

In European countries, there has been less opportunity for the dogs to fulfil their traditional function as flock protectors. Throughout Britain especially, even in the so-called 'wilderness' areas, public rights of way exist across most farmland; an encounter with a free-ranging Kangal Dog on guard would be alarming for hikers and would place the dog in a difficult situation, both psychologically and legally. However, the sensitive use of livestock guardians of various breeds has proved successful in many other European countries (Rigg, 2001, 2005) and Kangals have recently been introduced into habitats where wildlife conservation programmes have allowed wolves and bears to re-establish themselves.

Most Kangal Dogs living in western Europe, and many in North America, are kept as companions or domestic guardians, or for exhibition at dog shows—a role which, it must be said, not all of them take to with great enthusiasm.

Cedric Giraud and Aslan, Canadian representatives of the international Kangal family

Beginnings in Britain

It is known that a few dogs from Turkey were brought to the West long before any attempt was made to acknowledge a Turkish breed in any formal way.

Frank Buckland was a popular Victorian author and natural historian who in his lifetime collected many species from all over the world for his studies, often discussing them with Charles Darwin (with whom he had some differences of opinion). In 1863, he received a Turkish shepherd dog from a friend in Constantinople, Sir Edmund Hornby. In introducing this dog, Sir Edmund had written:

He is a splendid animal of the Koordish breed, and was procured from the district of Erzenhiern [Erzincan], from the shepherds. He is ten months old. His father guards a flock of sheep of 200 against any wolves and has killed several. His name is 'Arslan' or The Lion. ... His ears are cut, in order not to get them lacerated when fighting wolves, hyenas, the panther, or small black leopard etc.

Buckland's account of Arslan's arrival, 'Turkish guard dog from Trebizond', appeared in the British newspaper *The Field* in May 1863, with a line drawing by G.S. Melville. From the illustration it can be seen that Arslan was not a Kangal, but an example of what has recently become known as the Kars Dog of eastern Turkey, another of the country's breeds of shepherd dog.

Kars dogs and flocks on the range near Mount Ararat

The story of the Kangal Dog in Britain really begins, however, in 1965 when researcher-archaeologist Charmian Biernoff (later Steele, now Hussey) returned from field work in Turkey with two young dogs from the Konya region: Gazi, a male from the village of Bakırtolu, just east of the city, and his mate Sabahat from the neighbouring village of Hayıroğlu. Charmian and her husband David Biernoff had been part of a team of archaeologists led by James Mellaart excavating the prehistoric site at Çatalhöyük. A dog lover since childhood, Mrs Biernoff took a great interest in the distinctive working dogs in the area and was struck by the similarity between these local dogs and the representations of large, strong dogs in the Assyrian and Babylonian sculptures she had admired as a student. In fact, shortly after Mrs Biernoff and the two dogs had made the long journey home—overland, in an overflowing Citroën 2CV van—she received a letter from Dr Richard Barnett, then curator of the Department of Western Asiatic Antiquities at the British Museum, who wrote:

> I understand that you brought back some enormous Turkish sheep dogs with you. I am wondering what they are like in case they might be compared with the lion hounds on the Assyrian reliefs. If they are at all like them, could you spare me a photograph?

Assyrian relief showing dog and handler at the lion hunt (image reproduction courtesy of the Trustees of the British Museum)

Because the shepherd dogs that the Biernoffs saw on their travels were commonly called 'Karabaş' by the local people (*kara* = black, *baş* = head), this name was retained for the breed that Gazi and Sabahat were to found in England. It was also a name that had been quoted by travel writers in some classic descriptions of their encounters with fierce dogs in Asia Minor.

Gazi, Sabahat and their puppies

Shortly after their release from 6 months' quarantine, compulsory under UK law, Gazi and Sabahat were exhibited at Crufts Dog Show in London, where they attracted considerable interest. A year later, they produced their only litter, the first British-born pups of any Turkish breed. The dogs were accepted by the Kennel Club, at first as 'Anatolian Sheepdogs' and from 1968 until 1983 specifically as 'Anatolian (Karabash) Dogs'.

Arrivals in the USA

It may be that Charmian Biernoff was not the only, or indeed the first archaeologist to bring a Turkish shepherd dog to the West. Professor Rodney S. Young of the University of Pennsylvania, who directed the excavation of Phrygian tumuli at Gordion between 1950 and 1973 and famously discovered the spectacular tomb of King Midas, is believed to have taken dogs from Turkey home to the USA (Taylor, 1996). Whatever type of dogs these were, their progeny did not become part of today's US population of Turkish breeds, which was established by David and Judith Nelson in the late 1970s.

During the 4 years they spent in Turkey, the Nelsons focused initially on the large white flock guardian, the Akbaş Dog of western Turkey. This breed made a great impact when it was introduced into the USA as a working dog for farmers to use to protect sheep and goats on the range from attack by predators. Interest in this ancient method of reducing losses of livestock—to predation by coyotes, stray dogs, mountain lions and bears—had been stimulated by both economic and animal welfare concerns. Ranchers in the western states, for example, were losing an average of 8 per cent of their stock to predators, and farmers everywhere had resorted to the use of guns, poisons and snares, to the detriment of local wildlife.

In response to the growing environmental and conservation movement, in 1972 the US government banned the use of poisons for pest control and the search was on for an effective, non-lethal way to deal with predators of farm animals. Researchers looked to the 'Old World'—Europe and Asia—for livestock protection dogs of various (mainly white) breeds, in particular the Pyrenean Mountain Dog, the Italian Maremma and the Yugoslavian Sar Planinac. Quite large numbers of these dogs were imported and placed on farms and ranches through research programmes such as the US Sheep Experiment in Dubois, Idaho and the Livestock Dog Project at Hampshire College, Massachusetts.

In attempting to breed an all-purpose livestock guardian, some experiments produced crosses of the various breeds (Coppinger *et al.*, 1988), a policy which, unsurprisingly, was not welcomed by authorities in the dogs' country of origin or the breed societies established to protect their interests.

Many pups from the early American litters of Akbaş, the first of which arrived in 1978, were placed directly into working situations and their performance was monitored by the US Department of Agriculture and the various research organizations. Unfortunately, although the effectiveness of the Akbaş as a predator deterrent was indisputable, roughly half of the dogs died in road or other accidents, or they were maliciously shot. Quite apart from the animal welfare issues involved, these losses were unacceptable both financially (good livestock guardians cost money to produce and train) and for the survival of a genetically viable breeding population.

Following this experience, when the Kangal Dog came to the USA in 1985 the emphasis was on establishing and preserving a solid genetic base in selected breeding kennels, in family settings, or on small farms. There, the dogs could be observed and all aspects of their development monitored while a substantial population was gradually built up. Individuals from the generations that followed were then placed in livestock-guarding situations. By 1996 there were thought to be only about 20 Kangal Dogs working with sheep in the USA, compared to about 1500 Akbaş.

The Akbaş Dog of western Turkey

Akbaş Dogs and their sheep in Turkey

Kangals down under

Australia and New Zealand are two countries where, as in Turkey, large-scale extensive sheep production plays a major part in the national economy. In Australia particularly, predators cause major losses of livestock, and large sums of money have been invested in trying to prevent attacks by wild dogs, foxes and stray domestic dogs. In the mid-1980s British-bred 'Karabash' dogs were exported to a few forward-thinking smallholders in Australia and New Zealand who, through their interest in rare breeds, had heard of the reputation of the Turkish dogs as flock protectors.

However, it was not until 1996 that the direct link between Turkey and Australia was forged; Anne Nippers travelled to Turkey to study the breed at first hand, imported good breeding stock, and succeeded in gaining recognition for the Kangal Dog by the Australian National Kennel Council in 1998. Her lead was quickly followed in New Zealand by a few farmers of sheep and Angora goats who championed the breed, and the Kangal Dog was recognized by the New Zealand Kennel Club in 1999.

A variety of types in a class of Anatolian Shepherd Dogs at a British show

Besides using the dogs for sheep protection, enterprising Kangal owners in Australia are now using them in a new role, as guardians of valuable alpacas and llamas. This is an interesting twist on the established practice of using these camelids themselves to protect smaller livestock from foxes and dingoes. It is known that they have an innate dislike for canids generally (Jenkins, 2003); despite this, however, the new relationship with the Kangal seems to be working.

Northern Europe

Kangal Dogs have become particularly well established in Germany, Holland and France as a result of Turkish migrant workers bringing their dogs overland from home, and forming a network of owners and breeders.

Although many of these dogs have found a comfortable life with good owners, for others conditions suitable for Kangals have not been provided and they have fallen foul of anti-dog legislation, especially in some German states. Their owners have childhood memories of these noble dogs wandering free around their village, or the village of their fathers and grandfathers, but here the dogs have often been condemned to live, confused and frustrated, chained in a back yard or on the balcony of some cramped apartment block in an industrial town, with predictable results.

Sweden

Sweden has five species of wild predator that are protected by law: the golden eagle, lynx, wolf, bear and wolverine. By the turn of the 21st century populations of these species were very low and in 2002 the Swedish Environmental Protection Agency set up the Council for Predator Issues as a conservation initiative. This organization has been sponsoring research into ways of minimizing conflict between farmers and predators, conducting surveys and making funds available to compensate for losses of stock.

A young Kangal and her alpacas on the Australian farm of Zuhal Kuvan-Mills

Anne Voiry's dogs in France enjoy a game of chase

At work on pasture in a Swedish forest

Susanne Edlund's pair of Kangals in Sweden

Sweden once had its own breed of livestock guardian dog, the Dalbo, but this became extinct in the late 1800s. Like the Kangal in Turkey, the bravery of these dogs as protectors of home, family and flocks has been recorded in Swedish history; they too wore spiked iron collars for protection, some of which have been found in the areas where they used to work and are now exhibited in Dalsland Museum.

The tradition of using dogs as flock protectors has now been revived with the introduction of the Kangal Dog as part of the predator programme. Working as a non-lethal control, the dogs prevent attacks on stock while allowing the predator species to survive and reproduce. This in turn reduces the impact of poaching on their populations. In addition, by establishing a new community of Kangals, Sweden is helping to conserve another rare breed.

The project has had its challenges. Dogs are strictly regulated in Sweden: quarantine restrictions apply to dogs imported from a number of countries, including Turkey, and even the pet passport system involves a long qualifying period. As a result, the Kangal population is still relatively small and diagnosis of some inherited health problems has meant that the viable breeding population is even smaller.

Laws to protect wildlife species do not allow dogs to run freely off the lead; they may be used unleashed with stock only if part of a government programme and it has taken some persuasion to obtain permission for Kangals to work in their traditional way in Sweden. 'Right to roam' legislation that allows people free access across farmland is a further complication when dogs are on guard. Nevertheless, despite operating in a very different landscape from their natural Turkish habitat, the dogs have settled well. With careful guidance from breed enthusiasts, who are working with sheep societies and giving educational talks on the use of livestock guardians, Swedish Kangals are achieving good results for farmers and conservationists alike.

Africa

The latest journey taken by the Kangal Dog has been to southern Africa. Here, as on the Anatolian plateau in the summer months, vegetation is sparse and stock on commercial farms range over wide areas to find adequate grazing. Although the predators that threaten them are very different from those faced in America, the methods adopted by farmers to control them have been equally drastic: stock keepers have traditionally shot or trapped the big cats and hyenas that hunt on their land. It became clear in the 1990s that one particular species, the cheetah, was in danger of disappearing altogether from its important habitat in Namibia (Marker, 2005) so, following the lead of the researchers in the USA, conservationists set about introducing livestock-guarding dogs as a deterrent. In this way it has been possible to achieve a fairly sustainable co-existence of cheetahs, people and livestock in the region.

New pups arrive at the cheetah conservation project in Namibia

Turkish dogs were the favoured choice because of their physical adaptation to a hot, arid environment and because they were large and imposing enough to deter most predators, including cheetahs. The foundation stock for the dog-breeding programme in Namibia were imported from the USA and were not purebred Kangal Dogs, but later imports into other parts of southern Africa have been obtained directly from Turkish sources after careful evaluation of their working background.

If successful, this will be a doubly important conservation story. While safeguarding endangered wildlife species in a challenging environment, projects such as this can help to secure the future of this rare breed of livestock-guarding dog.

Setting off for work with the goats

A new trainee meets his teacher

Identity

There can be no doubt about the identity of Turkey's 'national' dog, or the regard that Turkish people have for it. The Kangal or Sivas-Kangal Dog is known throughout the country, to city dwellers and country folk alike, as a treasured part of the national heritage.

Ask almost any Turkish person about the big dogs used by the shepherds in Anatolia and they will describe the Kangal Dog. You will hear accounts of its superior strength and bravery against the wolf, told with great pride and enthusiasm. People who live and work in the towns, and also Turks who have moved abroad to start a new life, will often tell you how fondly they remember their father's or their grandfather's village where as toddlers they were allowed to ride on the back of the family's Kangal.

The dogs are regular participants in celebrations and parades held by cultural organizations such as the Turkish American Association in the USA. Children's Day in the Turkish community, 23 April, is one event where they often make a guest appearance, to the great delight of their young friends. The Kangal is a much-loved symbol of the home country, as much a part of the scene as the traditional song, dance, costume and cuisine enjoyed at these gatherings.

Proud owners often make beautifully decorated collars for their dogs to wear on special occasions. This collar incorporates the traditional Turkish nazar boncuğu, the lucky blue eye symbol worn to ward off evil

A Turkish icon

The Kangal Dog is such a source of national pride that it has twice featured on Turkish postage stamps, once in 1973 with its generic title of *çoban köpeği* and again in 1996 as *Kangal köpeği*. It is unfortunate that the artist who drew the image on the second stamp obviously had no personal knowedge of the Kangal Dog, but these stamps are none the less a tribute to the iconic status of the breed in its homeland.

In 2005 the Turkish Mint issued a commemorative silver 20-lira coin bearing the image of a *Kangal çoban köpegi* (Kangal shepherd dog).

A cultural treasure

In the brochures and books it produces for tourists, Turkey's Ministry of Culture and Tourism has for many years included the Sivas-Kangal Dog among the important features of the Central Anatolian region. There is also a whole gallery of photographs of the dogs on the Ministry's web pages dedicated to the breed.

Since the uncontrolled removal of many Kangals from the country in the 1970s and 1980s, Turkey has come to regard its 'national dog' in the same way that it protects archaeological treasures and works of art. The export of purebred Kangal Dogs (and Akbaş Dogs) is forbidden without government licence, and officials at air and sea ports, and at border posts on land, are watchful for infringements of this regulation. The rule does not apply, however, to other types of shepherd dog, which explains why the Anatolian Shepherd Dog population in the USA and Britain, for example, has been able to thrive. In November 2001 the Governorship of Kangal registered a patent for the Kangal Dog with the Turkish Patent Institute, as a means of establishing the regional provenance of the breed.

Ankara Zoo

This zoo is part of a large state farm established by Mustafa Kemal Atatürk in 1933. Besides its function as a public amenity it is an educational resource and a conservation centre for Turkey's indigenous species and breeds, among them the Angora cat.

The dogs at Ankara Zoo are a popular attraction for the visiting public. On weekends and holidays you will find families gathered around the Kangal enclosures, gazing in admiration at the big, leonine dogs as they saunter about or relax in the shade. If you eavesdrop on the conversation you are likely to hear stories being told to children about how brave 'Karabaş' chases away the wolves to protect his sheep.

These dogs have been bred and exhibited at the Zoo since 1959. This photograph was taken in the 1960s.

Government-controlled breeding centres have been established at Kangal town and the nearby state farm at Ulaş. Every dog's breeding, development and health record are charted, whether the animal is kept at the centres or based in a village and used for work. Pedigrees are recorded, and certificates of origin issued to owners of genuine Kangal Dogs.

Certificate of origin issued by the government breeding centre in Kangal town

Writings about Kangals

In writings old and new, a number of authors have described their encounters with Kangals.

Almost a hundred years ago, an English traveller, W.J. Childs, decided to walk from Samsun on the Black Sea coast of Turkey across the country to the shores of the Mediterranean in the south. His account of the journey, which took 5 months, is given in his book *Across Asia Minor on Foot*, published in 1917.

Childs seems to have had a particular aversion to dogs—unfortunate considering his frequent encounters with them—to which he actually devotes a section entitled 'Savage dogs'. Those he saw south of Sivas, not far from Kangal, certainly had the characteristic physique of the breed we know well, and perhaps the temperament too, when faced with a foreign intruder.

> *Beyond Kayadibi the country dogs were the largest and most savage of any I had met. In build they were like Newfoundlands, but larger, with black head or muzzle, yellow body and long curling tail. From nearly every flock that fed within a half-mile of the road a dog would presently detach itself and come lumbering across country to the attack. I had no doubt the shepherds set them on [us]—a well known trick of Turkish shepherds when a foreigner is passing—but I also more than half suspected Mehmet [driver of the cart that accompanied Childs] of somehow prompting the shepherds.*

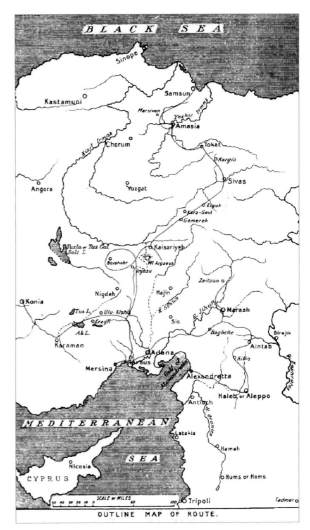

The route of Childs' journey, reported in his 1917 book

Kangals in modern novels

Louis de Bernières (author of *Captain Corelli's Mandolin*) once found himself besieged in his car by Kangal Dogs on guard, while he was researching his book *Birds Without Wings* (2004). This novel, set in western Turkey at the turn of the 20th century, is a moving portrayal of a community of Greek and Turkish neighbours caught up in the turmoil of those changing times. The landscape he describes, however, is timeless:

> *In March there are still rains and cold nights, quaggy patches of red and grey mud in the roadways, and the wind known as El Hossom whipping up the equinoctial gale that blows for eight long days. In the pastures the colossal Sivas Kangal mastiffs with their iron-spiked collars do nocturnal battle with subtle lynxes and desperate wolves, and the green sandpipers have not yet returned to the marshes and woods of the north.*

The breed makes a cameo appearance in the Inspector Ikmen series of detective novels by Barbara Nadel: in *Dance with Death* (2006) we meet 'the great yellow Kangal Dog, Zeytin', who guards her mistress, Nalan, at her cave house in Cappadocia.

Against the Storm (1990), a novel for children by Gaye Hiçyılmaz, is the story of a family who move to the capital, Ankara, from their village in the Anatolian countryside. With them goes the boy Mehmet's beloved Kangal Dog, Korsan:

> *He was a creamy white dog who stood elbow high beside Mehmet. He had been bred in another village and generations of his family had guarded the flocks of sheep and goats. They had fought off wolves and bears in the mountains and wild dogs and thieves on the plains. Korsan's ears had been cut short after his birth to save them from being torn in fights and this gave him a sad, puzzled expression.*

Books about dogs

The first authoritative all-breeds book in English that has given a true account of the situation regarding Turkish dogs is *Dogs: The ultimate dictionary of over 1000 dog breeds* (2001) by the renowned British zoologist, author and broadcaster Desmond Morris. This identifies Turkey's livestock protection dogs by the three distinct regional breeds: Akbaş, Kangal and Kars. At the same time it succinctly explains how the 'Anatolian Shepherd Dog' became established in the USA while remaining an unknown breed in Turkey.

Unsurprisingly, Turkish-language books describing the Kangal Dog are more numerous. Retired Turkish Army General and veterinarian Orhan Öncül gathered together his knowledge of dog training, nutrition and health, along with notes about a selection of breeds, Turkish and foreign, in his 1983 book *Sadık Dostumuz Köpekler Ailesi* (*The Dog Family: Our faithful friend*).

Later, as Kangal Dogs have become better known, a number of Turkish owners and breeders have published illustrated accounts of their own dogs and their experiences and views on the breed.

The Kangal Dog makes an appearance in public art just outside Istanbul. At an intersection along the busy road to Ankara, near the district of Darıca, stands a collection of life-size statues of a small flock of sheep with their dog. Originally the group included a statue of a shepherd too, resplendent in his felt cape (*kepenek*). Unfortunately, however, by 2009 he had been stolen, leaving the Kangal in sole charge of the flock.

Conferences

Perhaps the most successful exercise in establishing the identity of the Turkish livestock guardians for an international audience was the groundbreaking International Symposium on Turkish Shepherd Dogs held in Konya in 1996. The event brought together organizations and researchers from Turkey, the USA and western Europe, who reported on their experience of the different breeds. Professor O.C. Tekinşen, Dean of the Veterinary Faculty of Selçuk University, which hosted the symposium, stressed in his report the importance of recognizing the separate identity of the Turkish breeds:

> *The native shepherd dogs of Turkey are a Turkish national treasure. That is why we call them collectively, 'Turkish shepherd dogs'. Under this general rubric, we recognize at least three native Turkish shepherd dog breeds: the Kangal Dog of central Turkey, the Akbaş Dog of western Turkey, and the Kars Dog of eastern Turkey. The Turkish Tazı, as a sighthound, is in a separate class.*
>
> *We recognized the Kangal Dog many years ago—long before foreign dog breeders knew about them. They are a unique, regional Turkish dog breed whose purity must be protected. They occupy a special cultural and historical status in Turkish society.*

What's in a name?

Where Turkish dogs are concerned, the answer to this question is undoubtedly 'a great deal'. The debate that has prevailed about the naming of Turkish dogs stems from the same confused thinking among foreigners that produced the Anatolian Shepherd Dog breed. In Britain, for example, adherents to the name 'Karabash' claim that 'Kangal Dog' is a name that was invented for the breed by David Nelson in 1984.

So, in interviews with Sivas people while gathering information for this book, researchers were careful to include the open question 'If a stranger came to your village and asked "What breed of dog is that?", what would you tell them?' Back came the answer '*Kangal*', or '*Sivas-Kangal çoban köpeği*'. And what of their fathers' and grandfathers' time—what were the dogs called then? This was generally met with a note of exasperation in the reply '*Kangal*' (of course—whatever else?). Sometimes the name was combined with other words: *Kangal köpeği, Kangal iti* = Kangal dog (the old form *it* had been used by Turhan Kangal's family, and he testified to the use of the name *Kangal* for the breed in his great-grandfather's time); *Kangal cinsi* = Kangal breed (the answer given by the *muhtar* of Yelliceköyü, Veli Sönmez); *Kangal koyun köpeği* = Kangal sheepdog (in Karşiyaka district and Yeniceköyü, for example). But invariably *Kangal*.

'Karabaş' is often used by owners as the given name for their Kangal dog. It is a descriptive word meaning 'black head', so it equates in English to the use of, for example, Patch for a dog with a coloured area around one eye, Chalky or Snowy for white dogs, or Ginger and Smoky for cats of those colours. In fact, in Turkey quite a number of dogs, of any or no breed, are named Karabaş even though they do not have black faces.

There are several other very popular names for Kangals. Among them are Yaman (powerful), Duman (smoke), Ceylan (gazelle, often given to bitches) and elemental names such as Ateş (fire), Rüzgar (wind) and Bora (tempest). Unlike pet owners in more western countries, Turkish people generally avoid giving human names to their animals and they are rather shocked to hear that Turkish forenames have been used in that way by foreign Kangal owners, although it must be said they are rather less sensitive about calling their own dogs Bobby or Doris.

Since the Konya meeting, two International Kangal Dog Symposiums, focusing specifically on the breed, have taken place in Sivas province in conjunction with the traditional annual Kangal Festival. Hosted jointly by the Governor of Kangal, the provincial Governor and Sivas Cumhuriyet University, the first symposium was held in Kangal town in 2003, and the second at the Alacahan caravanserai in 2005. Both attracted a large international audience and brought together people whose interests ranged from the purely scientific, through rare breed and species conservation, to the dog show and pet fancy. This successful series of conferences is likely to continue as knowledge of the breed develops, and the proceedings of all three symposiums have proved to be a useful resource for researchers and breeders worldwide.

Mistaken identity

Considering the iconic status of the Kangal Dog in Turkey, and the impact the breed has had on the international scene as a working dog, it seems extraordinary that it remains unrecognized by the major dog registries in the USA and Europe. Ironically, the Anatolian Shepherd Dog—an invention of non-Turkish dog breeders—is recognized by the American Kennel Club (AKC), the multinational Fédération Cynologique Internationale and the Kennel Club in Britain. Despite representations from academics, historians, geneticists, veterinarians, farmers and breed specialists from Turkey and elsewhere, successive attempts to resolve this unsatisfactory situation have all failed (2009).

At the entrance to Kangal town stands a large statue of its famous dog

Of the three canine organizations, the Kennel Club has perhaps the least excuse for refusing to acknowledge the Kangal Dog, having once recognized the Anatolian (Karabash) Dog—ostensibly the same breed—on the basis of just such expert evidence in the 1960s. Even in those days of difficult communications and limited travel opportunities, it was accepted that Turkey had more than one indigenous breed of dog; the very construction of the English breed name was designed to allow for other specifics to appear in the parentheses, should they be imported later. Nowadays Turkey is a much more accessible place and anyone with an eye for a dog can see at first hand that the Anatolian Shepherd Dog is not a breed, merely a job description. Nevertheless, the Kennel Club persists in the notion that there is only one all-embracing breed of Turkish livestock guardian.

Over the years, Turkish authorities have been both polite and patient in indulging this mistaken approach. During the preparation of this book, in discussing the failure of other countries to recognize the Kangal Dog the response of most Turkish colleagues has been that it is 'their loss'. This view is shared by the academic community in Turkey who, according to Professor Mustafa Özcan of Istanbul University's Veterinary Faculty, have no doubts about the validity of the Kangal Dog as a breed in its own right. As one Governor of Kangal put it, 'They will learn, one day ...'. One can only wonder how long it will take for that day to come. The Rare Breeds Survival Trust requires a minimum period of existence of 75 years for a breed to 'qualify' as a breed (Alderson, 1978). While direct evidence from Turkey would put the Kangal Dog on safe ground according to these criteria, the Anatolian Shepherd Dog, invented in the 1980s, should have to wait until at least the mid-2050s to come of age.

'One day ...'

A breed apart

While some foreign agencies have chosen to dismiss the testimony of both Turkish academics and the people who have direct experience of working with Kangals, other respected visitors to central Anatolia have taken a more considered view. They have contributed observations from their field work to the debate about type and breed.

Dr Sebastian Payne is a British zoo-archaeologist specializing in the origins and history of animal domestication, whose work includes the study of animal bones from excavations in Turkey and the eastern Mediterranean. In 1984 he shed light on the different types of Turkish livestock protection dogs in a letter to John McDougall, then Chairman of the Kennel Club.

The working dogs ...

... that I have seen used by Turkish sheep- and goat-herders (sheep and goats are often herded together) on the central and western plateau do conform, in a broad sense, to a rather variable general type: they tend to be large and heavy, with a relatively heavy head and shoulder, the coat is dense but not very long, and they are fast, strong and, on meeting strangers, tend to be vocally aggressive. These are all qualities that are valuable in the work they do—they are not sheepdogs in the sense that we think of them in this country, but are flock guard-dogs. Breeding is usually not controlled but puppies that are weak, or are thought to be less suitable for the work, are quickly weeded out; there is very considerable variation, both within village and from area to area in size, build, shape and colour. Calling these dogs a breed would, I would have thought, be to define a breed much too loosely and widely. Turkish villagers themselves usually distinguish local rough-bred animals (whether sheep, cattle or dogs), which they call 'yerli' (of the place, local), from more highly bred animals of named breeds, often of foreign origin. In this context these working dogs are thought of as 'yerli'. They are often called 'çoban köpekleri' (shepherd dogs), but this simply describes their function, as distinct, for instance, from 'av köpekleri' (hunting dogs); as the dominant type is large headed and has a black mask, they are also often called 'kocabaş' (big head) or 'karabaş' (black head)—terms that again generally have no implication other than descriptive. Some villagers try to improve their dogs by controlling breeding, but there's no generally agreed 'breed description' that they are aiming at—they are simply trying to produce a dog that does the work better, or will command a better price from other people who will also use the dog for the same work.

By contrast, the same villagers talk of 'Sivas köpekleri' (Sivas dogs) as a distinct and highly bred breed; they will talk of buying in and breeding from a Sivas dog in the same way that they will talk of buying in a Merino ram, or a Holstein bull. ... dogs that are pointed to in the villages as resembling Sivas dogs, or having Sivas dog blood, tend to be particularly heavy in the head and shoulder, to have a fairly short and dense cream or fawn coat and a black mask (the ears are probably also black, but are normally cropped) and a strongly curled tail, resembling the Sivas dogs I have seen in Ankara Zoo.

Subject to the reactions of Turkish dog-breeders, it seems to me that while there is every reason for the Kennel Club to recognize the Sivas dog (or Sivas-Kangal dog as it now seems to be called in veterinary circles—Kangal is a small town near Sivas with a reputation for these dogs) as a breed, in line with Turkish usage, there is on the other hand little justification for recognising small groups of animals recently selected from within the more variable rough-bred working dog population as distinct breeds, at least until they are better established.

(Payne, 1984)

Anthony Fitzherbert, a senior agricultural advisor with the Food and Agriculture Organization of the United Nations, was working in eastern Turkey as a consultant to the World Bank when one of the authors of this book asked him about indigenous dog breeds. In 1984 he wrote from Erzurum:

Dear Mrs Mellor

I do not know if you ever received my letter, written just before my departure for eastern Turkey, but this is really to follow that one up with a little more information on the Kangal shepherd dogs.

The dogs that I spoke of in the letter, of which I had been told last year as being used for pit combat, are something different, and I have not been able to find out anything more about them. However, as both our senior vet and one of our district agricultural officers come from the Sivas area they have been able to tell me a bit about the 'Kangal çoban köpeği'. They are apparently mainly found in the district of Kangal which is part of Sivas province. … They are reputed to be of more than exceptional intelligence and though they do not actually round up the flocks in the way we use sheep dogs, they are exceptionally good guard dogs and a single shepherd or even (so they say) a child can herd a flock of sheep where in other places two adults are needed. They are reputed to be extremely courageous and quite a match for marauding packs of wolves.

This letter not only illustrates the distinction drawn between Kangals and other types of working shepherd dogs, it mentions dogs of yet another type, those used in combat. It is not surprising that Anthony Fitzherbert was unable to find out very much about these dogs, for dog fighting tends to be a fairly clandestine business, both in Turkey and elsewhere (more of this in Chapter 10). The preferred type for fighting is more aggressive than the Kangal Dog and is more heavily built, with thicker leg bones and a more massive head with heavy jowls—in general, more of a mastiff construction. There are areas of Turkey where pockets of this type of dog can be found.

This leads one to speculate whether there may be an ancestral link here between these dogs and the mastiffs of the Assyrians ('Don't think, bite!') discussed in the early chapters of this book.

'Junior handling' at the Kangal Festival

Shepherd boy with his Kangal

Health, care and ownership

Owning a Kangal Dog is a privilege. Most of the time it is also a pleasure!

People will often tell you that once having had a Kangal they can never think of keeping another breed, so you could say that they get under your skin.

It is hard to be precise about the qualities that make these dogs so special, but this chapter will try to describe some facets of their character and outline some of the responsibilities that owners undertake when they decide to share a life with them.

Hasan Babacan and one of his favourite Kangals

Companion Kangals

The term 'companion dog' has recently replaced 'pet dog' in our vocabulary. Companionship is important: it is unfair to keep a Kangal Dog in a domestic situation if it is going to be shut out of the home all the time. In a working environment the dog has a job to do and livestock for company: at home, owners have to make up for that by sharing their own time, space and family.

Keeping a Kangal Dog as a companion makes for a rewarding relationship, provided that all members of the household understand and respect the nature of the breed.

Sultan helping Altuğ Tahtakılıç to read the paper

Marianne Gaunt introduces Dixie to their newly arrived Jack Russell puppy

Animal partnerships

Properly introduced, a Kangal will live happily with other pets, including other dogs provided the Kangal is allowed to be the 'alpha' dog. This means that other naturally dominant breeds may, to put it mildly, be uneasy housemates, whereas the easier-going breeds will be good companions and will enjoy being looked after by their big Turkish friend. Generally speaking, male–female partnerships work best.

The breed's natural instinct to protect what it sees as 'belonging' to its household becomes more obvious as the dog matures. Puppies will tease the family cat and chase chickens, so vulnerable pets will have to be protected in these early stages, especially if there is no older dog to learn from, but in time a Kangal will regard them all as part of the family and therefore will watch over them. Visiting cats, dogs, birds and other creatures will need to beware, however, because Kangals are very good at distinguishing between what does and does not belong on their territory.

Aysun shares her bed with the family cat

Pack leadership

In a domestic setting some owners experience problems with over-dominant behaviour in adolescent Kangals (around the age of 18 months to 3 years). If this happens, it is useless and cruel to try to bully the dog into submission; that will only result in a resentful and potentially aggressive adult dog.

There are certain ground rules to apply from the day your puppy comes home, which will establish your position as 'pack leader' while avoiding a battle of wills. These methods apply to any companion dog but especially to large, headstrong breeds like the Kangal. It is important to maintain a calm but superior position in relation to your dog, For example: do not allow it to sit or lie on your furniture—that is your privilege; keep your eye level above that of the dog's; always lead the way through doorways or up stairs. Natural pack leaders do not respond to attention-seeking behaviour so, hard as it may be, new owners should learn to ignore demands for attention so that treats and affection are always given on their own terms.

Pack leader ignoring demands for attention

Human partnerships

Relationships with humans are much more complex, not because Kangals are 'difficult', for they are remarkably straightforward animals with very simple, but important needs. It is the human component that is difficult. Some people, particularly obedience enthusiasts, are inclined to enjoy imposing their will on a dog (although they are less inclined to shoulder the blame when things go wrong) and this is a breed that is used to thinking for itself. On the other hand, treating a Kangal puppy like an oversized teddy bear can backfire too. Kangals are strong-minded, independent and can seem aloof, but they bond naturally to people who care for them. It is the strength and nature of this bond that make the partnership unique.

This is not the breed for someone who likes a dog to fawn over them, cling to their heels and constantly look to them for instruction. That said, while a Kangal Dog may not follow its owners everywhere, it will want to keep an eye on where they are and what they are doing. Kangals may not always seem to be paying attention but they are observant and inquisitive.

Home truths

Here are some important practical considerations for anyone thinking of sharing their home with a Kangal Dog.

First of all, these are large, active dogs that need plenty of living space. Everything you have read in this book about their development over the centuries, and the environment in which they do the job they are designed for, explains why this should be. They are not city dogs and they will soon become frustrated, noisy, confused and even destructive if closely confined alone for any length of time. A large secure space is ideal, with another animal or human for company most of the time, and plenty of walks on the lead to enable them to understand what lies beyond their boundaries.

Kangals will guard as far as they can see and hear. They do not bark unnecessarily, but they do bark at unfamiliar sights or sounds. So, if its territory is next to a footpath where strangers frequently come and go, a dog will sound its presence at every approach. This can be difficult to live with, for the owner and for neighbours, and it is unfair for the dog to be constantly scolded for what is after all normal behaviour in a guarding breed.

Like their working Turkish counterparts, Kangal Dogs in any situation become more alert and will guard more vociferously after dark. They also patrol—not constantly, but from time to time—overnight. Therefore owners should not be surprised if several times during the night they hear their dog get up, saunter from one place to another and flop heavily down, most probably across a doorway or against a door (favourite location).

In the dog's outdoor space a weatherproof shelter should be provided into which it can escape from showers or extreme heat. Indoors, as with any house dog, a Kangal should have its own bed or rug to sleep on, or a box that can also double as a travel crate—a particularly good idea if there are plans to go travelling together. While Kangal Dogs will delight in sunbathing on concrete or paving, or stretching out on a tiled kitchen floor, they also need a softer surface to curl up on for part of the time. Being heavy dogs, they will develop callouses on elbows and hocks if they do not have this option. In a working situation, Turkish dogs dig themselves comfortable hollows in the earth to lie in so, gardeners beware, a companion dog is likely to do the same in its owner's garden.

While a weatherproof shelter is important, there is no guarantee that a Kangal will always use it. This dog is fast asleep in the nest she has made in the snow

Boundaries

Secure fences are essential. Kangals are no respecters of boundaries and will use as wide a radius as they are allowed. They are also good diggers and jumpers, which means in a domestic situation that good fencing is required, to a height of 2 metres and with a solid base. In a rural location or on the farm, electric fencing will usually deter escapers, although the current needs to be adjusted so as not to harm the dog.

People have had mixed results with so-called invisible fencing, where the 'hot wire' runs underground. With both conventional and invisible electric fencing, a Kangal that is sufficiently provoked to give chase to a perceived threat may well just grit its teeth and go over, regardless. Deer fencing, designed to cope with animals that jump, works well but might need to be supplemented by stock fencing or a similar grid laid flat along the ground to prevent dogs from digging out. (The photograph at the beginning of this chapter shows the use of a wire grid at ground level.)

Whichever form of perimeter fencing is selected, owners will still need to ensure the safety of legitimate callers at their house, such as postal workers or couriers, so the route to their door needs to be secure. This could require some careful garden design, bearing in mind that Kangals cannot be expected to ignore an open gate. On no account should Kangals be kept chained or tethered; it is a cruel practice and dogs that become entangled in a running-chain are easily injured.

Guarding the lamb paddock on a farm in Washington state, USA. An electric line runs above the stock fencing

Care of working dogs

The tough working life of these dogs in Turkey has already been described in this book at some length, and they have also adjusted to quite a wide range of environments in other countries.

Like any working dog, Kangals are expected to attend to their flocks in all weathers. In high summer they will pace themselves to cope with the heat, moving slowly and steadily and taking advantage of any cool or shady spots along their route. Thirst does not seem to be a major concern to them, for even after a long trek they will not rush to water but simply take up what they need in a fairly relaxed way, sometimes cooling off in a stream or trough, all the time keeping an eye on the flock.

Cooling off in a water trough on a hot day

Digging in Swedish snow

Kangal Dogs love snow: they will chase about in it, dig nests in it and eat it. They appear to be stimulated by the fact that moving objects can be seen from a distance against the white landscape and are particularly watchful in these conditions.

What they do not enjoy is rain. Early spring in Anatolia can bring cold, wet weather and this is a time when the dogs prefer to spend the minimum time in the open. Sheep still have to be moved, however, and this tends to be done at more of a trot than an amble, head and tail down. This aversion to water has also been noticed by owners of companion Kangals, who have found (sometimes to their relief) that the family dog is no more anxious to go walking in the rain than they are.

Looking out over a Canadian snowfield

Living with stock

Turkish dogs grow up around and among sheep, alongside the older dogs in the village. In other countries where the working environment is different, livestock owners have to play a more active role in encouraging young Kangals to behave appropriately around stock, as mentioned in Chapter 5. Mistakes have sometimes been made when placing youngsters in a working situation. It is unfair to expect a Kangal puppy or an inexperienced youngster to understand from the outset how to behave with livestock, particularly if there are no other dogs from which to learn. The inbuilt affinity is in place, certainly, and the character traits of this breed are there to be developed, but without time and guidance any dog is likely to get into trouble when it is first confronted by a flock of sheep or goats.

The bonding process is helped if the dog's living quarters are shared with, or alongside the stock. In Turkish villages during the winter months the dogs will often spend the night in the barns with the sheep, or will shelter just outside the door or on the roof. Most owners of working Kangals in other countries provide a weatherproof kennel either in the sheep paddock or next to it, although very often in bad weather the dog will simply settle in beside the stock if it has access to their housing.

American Kangals, settling in beside their sheep

Health

The generally robust constitution of today's Kangal Dog is the legacy of generations of 'survival of the fittest' in its work setting, as described in Chapter 4. Over the centuries shepherds have kept the strongest pups in the litter as potentially good workers; those dogs that survive to maturity are the ones that produce the next generation, and so the cycle continues. This process of what might be described as assisted natural selection favours not only the physically fit dogs but those with the temperament best suited to their function. A shepherd will not tolerate a dog that worries the sheep, or fails to guard, or runs away from predator threats, or shows aggression to its owner and family. So it is easy to see how, as a breed, the physical and psychological traits for which the Kangal is famous have become imprinted.

Very few breed-specific health problems have been identified in Kangals, although there are some heritable problems that they share with other large breeds.

Ear infections are common in drop-eared breeds and are often related to seasonal allergies

Sensitivity to anaesthetic drugs

Veterinarians in Turkey and elsewhere have observed that particular care needs to be taken when Kangal Dogs are anaesthetized for surgery. The problem is not one of allergic reaction to the drugs, but rather it concerns the risk of overdose, particularly in the use of the very common, cheap intravenous anaesthetic, ketamine. Losses of Kangals during routine operations have resulted in vets advising against the use of this drug if possible, but unfortunately not all clinics, especially in rural practices, are suitably equipped to intubate animals for surgery. (A recommended regime (2008) is, first, intravenous Diazepam as a muscle relaxant, followed by Propofol to induce anaesthesia and then maintenance with inhaled isofluorane.) Where ketamine is the only option, approximately half the normal dosage—calculated, as for many other drugs, according to the weight of the animal—has proved adequate in Kangals. However, the message from experienced vets is close observation of the patient throughout surgery and 'topping up' the medication if necessary.

Allergies

Some Kangals in Turkey have been found to be allergic to certain synthetic suture material, in particular polyglactin 910, used for absorbable sutures. The reaction takes the form of inflammation and swelling around the site of the stitches. In cases where this has occurred, resuturing with polydioxanone (PDS), also an absorbable synthetic, has produced no reaction.

Turkish veterinarians have also observed contact allergies to materials used in collars, such as nickel, especially in guarding dogs where the collar has been worn tight against the skin.

In fact, allergies in general appear to be on the increase, not only in animals but in humans, especially children. There is also a genetic component—allergies tend to run in families. This means that in the relatively small population of a rare breed of animal, one breeding line may make up a large proportion of the total and a family problem may mistakenly be seen as a breed characteristic.

Tongue-tie

This is condition where the frenulum, the membrane below the tongue, fastens the underside of the tongue to the base of the mouth. In an adult dog the condition is particularly visible when the dog is panting, because the tongue is unable to hang out of the open mouth; lapping is also difficult, although it must be said that most dogs learn to drink and feed efficiently despite this deformity. The membrane is very fine in the first few days of life and the condition can be easily corrected under mild anaesthetic by a veterinarian. Not all puppies in a litter may be affected, but tongue-tie is an inherited condition that should be checked for in a breeding programme.

Allergies and vaccinations

For many years there has been a great deal of debate as to whether chronic allergies experienced in a few Kangals, particularly skin irritation in British dogs, could be attributable to the effect on the immune system of routine vaccinations against diseases such as distemper and leptospirosis. Some have speculated that this might be a more common phenomenon in the more 'primitive' breeds such as this one. However, allergies such as atopic dermatitis are increasingly common in a large number of dog breeds.

Whether there is a link to vaccines or not, veterinarians have recently re-examined the need for annual 'boosters' to routine vaccinations for companion animals generally.

In guidelines published in 2007, the World Small Animal Veterinary Association (WSAVA) acknowledged the need to 'reduce the "vaccine load" on individual animals in order to minimize the potential for adverse reactions to vaccine products'. The key message of its report was: 'We should aim to vaccinate every animal, and to vaccinate each individual less frequently'.

(WSAVA, 2007)

Health issues in working dogs

Working Kangals in central Anatolia are exposed to a range of health challenges that their counterparts in the suburbs do not face. The most obvious threat is injury, from encounters with predators such as wolves and stray dogs, and particularly with wild boar, which can do far worse damage. Then there is trauma caused by the wear and tear of everyday life, such as leg and foot injuries from the mountainous terrain and the subsequent risk of infection.

Infectious diseases are a major health danger to rural dogs. Most of the risks are avoidable, but at a price which poorer owners cannot pay and many others are not prepared to pay. Vaccines against the major infectious diseases are available, even in rural Turkey, but most village dogs go unprotected. Rabies vaccination is compulsory in Turkey. Other viral diseases such as distemper and parvovirus are common; it is only the infrequency of contact between village communities that prevents outbreaks from becoming epidemics.

Parasitic diseases take a very severe toll, especially on puppies. Heavy infestations of roundworms damage the immature gut of puppies, who die from internal bleeding that is often mistaken for parvovirus. A simple, inexpensive worming regime would prevent this, especially if lactating bitches were included, for they are part of the cycle of infection. The needs of bitches generally are much neglected in Turkey, it must be said, despite the fact that they are often the most attentive flock guardians and, importantly, the teachers of the next working generation.

Other internal parasites are also easily controllable by routine dosing: debilitating tapeworm (*Taenia*), fatal heartworm (*Dilofilaria*) and *Echinococcus*, the agent of hydatid disease, dangerous to both sheep and humans.

Haemorrhagic gastroenteritis (HGE), whether caused by parasitic or other infections, is the most common cause of death in puppies. Owners hoping for a large, impressive Kangal may not be aware that persistent diarrhoea in puppyhood almost always means that the dog will fail to grow to its full size and strength. Treating this problem promptly and correctly is as important for future growth and development as good feeding.

Ectoparasites (such as fleas, ticks and mites) also carry infectious diseases. Sarcoptic and demodectic mange affect both dogs and livestock, so are a production problem for farmers as well as a cause of suffering to the dog. Sheep ticks are hosts for the agents of ehrlichiosis and babesiosis, debilitating and often fatal diseases for dogs. They can also carry the notorious viral disease Crimean Congo haemorrhagic fever, which is not fatal to animals but claimed the lives of 92 people in north and central Turkey in just 5 years; the death toll continues to mount. These parasites are much more difficult to deal with, because control involves not only treating the coat of the dog and the other animals that carry them, but the environment in which the immature stages of the cycle develop.

Heritable problems shared with other breeds

The skeletal problems encountered in other large breeds also occur to some extent in the Kangal Dog. These include hip dysplasia (HD) and osteochondritis dissecans (OCD), diseases of the joints that are known to have a genetic component but are also influenced by the growing dog's environment and diet. Risk factors are very rapid growth, excess weight, and extreme exercise, especially at a stage when the young dog's joints and the soft tissue supporting them are still developing.

Other inherited conditions such as entropion (a deformity of the eyelid) and umbilical hernia do occasionally occur. In a small gene pool, such as exists in countries outside Turkey, hereditary problems are a serious matter and it is particularly important for breeders to act responsibly. The Kangal Dog population in Turkey benefits from much wider genetic resources and also, as mentioned previously, from farmers having selected generations of dogs that are effective workers. However, problems still arise, especially where breeders are tempted to breed for size rather than soundness. HD screening is not yet routinely performed in Turkey but research is planned (2008) to assess the hip status of working dogs in the Sivas area.

Examining a dog at the Kangal Dog Research Centre at Cumhuriyet University, Sivas

Combing out a shedding undercoat during the twice-yearly moult

General care

From the point of view of routine grooming, this is a very easy breed to look after. The short, dense, weatherproof coat is almost self-cleaning. A Kangal Dog can return from a muddy expedition, curl up in a dry corner and an hour or two later most of the dried mud will have dropped off in a neat patch on the floor. This thick, double coat is normally shed completely twice a year, a process that takes a good 3 weeks to complete and can produce enough moulted hair to fill a dustbin.

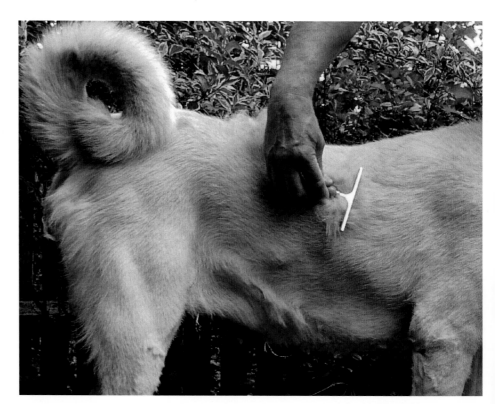

As long as the dog receives sufficient exercise on a hard surface, claws will wear down naturally. However, in older dogs that are less active, or where exercise is mainly on grass, strong clippers or a coarse nail file will be needed to keep claws in trim. Many Kangals have hind dewclaws, and in some cases double dewclaws. These do not wear down (although some dogs are obliging enough to nibble at them) and may become ingrown, so they do need regular attention.

It is a good idea to go through the routine of a light pedicure regularly from puppyhood, just to get dogs into the habit of being handled. It may be necessary to deal with thorns or other paw injuries later in life, when a Kangal Dog weighs 60 kg and is harder to restrain. The same goes for cleaning ears and checking teeth, all useful practice for visits to the vet. Like any drop-eared breed, Kangals are susceptible to ear infections; the first signs are persistent head shaking or carrying the head tilted to one side. Once infection sets in it can be very difficult and expensive to cure, so this calls for professional treatment with antibiotics as soon as possible.

The owner of this Kangal Dog keeps its double dewclaws under control with a file designed for acrylic fingernails. Note the 'extra toe' often seen in Kangals

Diet

Food scraps brought for working dogs on the mountainside

The staple diet of working Kangals in Turkey is *yal*, a mash of barley flour mixed with water, or with whey from cheesemaking during the sheep milking season. This mix is usually fed to the dogs in the morning before they set out with the flocks and often the shepherd will feed other food scraps to them later in the day.

There is little meat in the diet of either the dogs or the villagers. In wintertime the dogs are sometimes fed in the barns or, if outside, their ration is given in smaller portions during the day because any left in the bowl will quickly freeze.

Puppies are weaned on to cow's or sheep's milk with *yal* when their mother's milk starts to fail after 3–4 weeks. By this time, the bitch will have started to regurgitate her own food for them, as an introduction to solids. A wise shepherd understands that a dog has to be fed well if it is going to work well, so whatever extra nutrition the family can spare, such as eggs, yoghurt or meat scraps, goes to the growing dog.

In urban areas of Turkey where Kangals are kept as family dogs or to guard property, the most convenient way to feed them is with commercially produced pet food, most often 'complete' dry kibble. As in any other country, the quality of these products can be very variable and the nutritional content of the cheaper supermarket brands may be poor. Vets will tend to recommend the better-known imported brands, formulated scientifically to achieve what is perceived to be the correct balance of nutrients. Whether the balance is necessarily correct for dogs such as the Kangal is another question.

Many owners in Europe and the USA suspect, for example, that the generally high protein content of these formula feeds may lead to problems such as hyperactivity and skin problems in this breed. Considering that the Kangal evolved on a low-protein diet it seems quite possible that the composition may, indeed, not be suitable. In any case, these imported products are extremely expensive and beyond the budget of many Turkish families.

Aslan, in Canada, waits patiently for his dinner. His owners prefer to give him a combination of home-made and proprietary food

Feeding time for a Kangal litter at 6 weeks of age

Generally, a compromise involving a combination of simple ingredients (cereal, vegetables, meat) and some proprietary dog food appears to work well. Supplementation with extra vitamins and minerals should only be attempted under professional advice; it is very easy, especially in a large, fast-growing breed such as this, to make mistakes that will damage the dog's physical development (Demirci, 2005).

Whether owners opt for a home-made fresh/raw diet or one of the better-quality manufactured feeds, moderation and a good balance are the key principles. Growing puppies need plenty of protein, but adult Kangals do not need or benefit from high-protein feed. Slow, steady growth is much safer for good bone and joint development than allowing pups to gain a lot of weight quickly from too much starch, which can result in strain on the joints and deformation at the growth plates. It is best not to listen to folklore when it comes to nutrition: if you are concerned that your dog is not receiving enough of anything, get the opinion of a good veterinarian.

Growing up

Compared to most large breeds the lifespan of the Kangal Dog is surprisingly long. With good care it is not unusual for Kangals to live to the age of 12–14 years. However, it takes all of the first 3 years for them to reach maturity, and probably rather longer in the case of males.

Kangal litters are usually quite large, comprising six to eight puppies on average but sometimes many more. Given the opportunity, their mother will disappear to a secret location and excavate a cave in which to give birth, perhaps underneath an outbuilding or hedge. This is a very strong instinct, even in bitches that have lived all their lives in a domestic situation, and something that owners need to anticipate as the due date approaches. In the villages, when a particularly large litter is born it is common for other bitches in the family to begin lactating, even though they have no puppies of their own, and to share the feeding. No other dogs, and only the most trusted humans, will be allowed to approach.

A litter of Kangal puppies at one day old

Early puppyhood

At birth Kangal puppies are dark grey in colour, usually with a pronounced dark stripe along the spine.

Depending on the number in the litter, a good-sized puppy will weigh nearly 900 g at birth; by the time it is ready to go to its new home at 7 weeks it is likely to have reached 10 kg.

At that stage its coat colour will have started to clear to almost the adult fawn and will be thick and dense with a distinctive velvety texture. The black pigmentation on the mask and ears often fades at about 6 weeks, but returns after a few months when the adult coat develops.

Seven weeks old

Like their human counterparts, adolescent Kangals seem to be 'all arms and legs' for a long time. Different parts of the puppy seem to grow at different rates: it seems to take forever for the dog's head to catch up with the size of its ears, or for its legs to grow in proportion to its paws. In fact, the whole process of growing to full height takes nearly 2 years, and the skull and torso continue to broaden and mature for even longer than that.

During this period of rapid growth, care should be taken to discourage activities that put particular strain on the joints and tendons, such as jumping or scrambling over obstacles or racing up and down stairs. Controlled, steady exercise is preferable and safer at this stage.

An adolescent Kangal

Young female

Young male

Mature female

Mature male

(Dis)obedience

Although some owners have had a degree of success with agility classes, generally speaking Kangal Dogs are not good candidates for obedience training, as the Turkish army quickly found when it tried out the idea. This does not mean that Kangals are stupid; on the contrary, they are very good at 'reading' their owners and will go along with reasonable requests. However, do not expect them, for instance, to retrieve an object more than once (if you throw it away twice you clearly don't want it back), or to stop in their tracks if they are seeing a strange animal off the premises.

A young agility team in Sweden

In an urban environment it is therefore easy to understand why experienced owners advise against exercising this headstrong breed off the lead in public places such as parks. A free-running Kangal could get itself into trouble by chasing away another dog or, simply by its sheer size and weight, accidentally frightening a child or elderly person.

Early learning

In a working situation, whether in Turkey or elsewhere, the best trainer for a young Kangal apprentice is an older dog. Companion Kangals too will learn good behaviour from an older, sensible dog (of any breed) in the household. Puppies are easy to housetrain and quickly understand the daily routines of their owners, becoming accustomed to everyday sights and sounds.

They benefit from early socialization so, as soon as vaccinations are complete, puppy playgroups are a good idea.

It might take some time for a puppy to overcome travel sickness, something to be prepared for on car trips, but it is worth persevering because coping with a queasy puppy is much easier than with a full-sized Kangal that travels badly.

As the puppy matures, it is important to make a point of introducing it to visitors who come to the home, rather than keeping it separate from them. This kind of early socialization pays dividends in later life and will not compromise a Kangal's natural guarding instincts, which start to develop at the age of about 12 months. Once that stage is reached, strangers will be viewed with suspicion and warned off unless welcomed by the dog's owner.

Dogs and the law

The law governing dogs and dog owners varies from one country to another. It is a sad fact that in some countries Turkish breeds are on the 'dangerous' or restricted list, so owners need to be aware of the breed's status in their country or state, and to observe whatever controls apply. Should there be an incident involving a Kangal Dog, it is almost guaranteed that it will be the big dog, and not the smaller one, or indeed the human element, that will be blamed.

Local laws may require dogs to wear some means of identification. European dogs belonging to a pet passport scheme will be microchipped, a technology that still has its opponents but in many ways works well. However, it does require a microchip reader and access to a database to identify a dog, so a name tag with a telephone number is often the quickest and most efficient way to trace the owner. Given that Kangals are renowned escape artists, tend not to come when called, and can cover long distances very quickly, traceability is something to bear in mind. In addition, insurance cover that will provide for third party damage, injury to the dog itself, and legal costs, is a worthwhile investment.

Over the years a number of large guarding breeds have gained notoriety as a result of irresponsible breeding and ownership, and have suffered from sensational media reporting. It is up to Kangal owners and breeders to ensure that the reputation of this breed does not follow that course.

Breeding

Because the Kangal Dog is a rare breed beyond its home country, there is often pressure on owners to breed from their dog. For the reasons explained in this chapter, before going ahead it is important to be sure that both of the dogs involved are sound, physically and temperamentally. Under no circumstances should a bitch be bred from before the age of 2 years.

Veterinary support must be on hand during whelping and is essential for postnatal checks, and this can be costly; expenditure on food, bedding, worming, vaccinations, advertising and, if available, registration will soon mount up. There are a number of questions to address before taking the plunge. First of all, are there enough good homes waiting for the puppies? Kangal litters may be large: do you have the spare time and the facilities to look after any pups that are not homed promptly? What if the new owners find they cannot cope with a boisterous, unruly young dog? Or if their circumstances change and they cannot keep it? Breeders have a moral responsibility to take back the dogs they have bred, in such an eventuality. Although Kangal puppies are a real joy, they are also a great responsibility.

The future

What does the future hold for the Kangal Dog? To answer this question we need to consider the prospects for the breed in its homeland in central Anatolia and also in other countries. We need to look at the future of the breed in its traditional role as a flock guard as well as its use in other roles and as a companion dog.

The working environment of the Kangal has extended beyond its homeland in recent years to include a number of other countries. Its guarding instincts and skills are being used to protect various types of farmed animals from predators, sometimes as a vital part of wildlife conservation schemes for threatened species. This trend seems likely to continue.

Kangal puppy at a breed society meeting in Germany

The Kangal Dog itself is under threat in various ways. The decline of sheep rearing in its traditional homeland means the loss of a role for the working dog. Various schemes are in progress to improve the farming situation in central Anatolia, some of which are linked to Turkey's possible accession to the European Union.

Another more sinister threat is cross-breeding with other types of dog to achieve a larger, more aggressive animal. This practice is often linked to organized dog fighting, which although illegal in Turkey continues clandestinely. Fortunately, the Kangal Dog has supporters both within Turkey and elsewhere who are concerned for the welfare of the breed.

Safeguarding a traditional role

Recent years have seen the involvement of international organizations in local farming projects that directly or indirectly may help to secure the future of the Kangal Dog in its working capacity.

Some initiatives, such as the EU co-sponsored Sheep Husbandry Project described in Chapter 6, have focused on improving sheep production in the Sivas area, thereby aiming to reverse the decline seen in recent decades. If this investment in farming and education revitalizes sheep rearing in the region it will bring with it a continued need for flock protection dogs. And, as Turhan Kangal says, 'Without the sheep, the dog is nothing'.

A chilly May morning on the road just outside Sivas: this shepherd walks his flock of sheep and goats out to find grazing

United Nations Development Programme (UNDP)

In 2004 the Small Grants Programme of the UNDP funded a project called 'Protection of Wildlife through Use of Kangal Shepherd Dogs in Traditional Animal Husbandry'. The stated aim of the project was to protect the traditional role of Kangal Dogs as a working breed, using them as a non-lethal method of dealing with livestock predators that might otherwise have been poisoned or shot.

Based in Haymana district near Ankara, the 2-year project received a grant of $35,000 to support the breeding of healthy Kangal puppies, appropriate preparation for a working life, and their placement in local farms. Improvements were made to the facilities on the farm at the centre of the scheme, Doğa Farm, and information and advice were made available to participating farmers in the form of leaflets, support visits from the project team, media broadcasts and a web site (UNDP, 2006).

A Haymana shepherd works with some of the Kangal Dogs that have been placed on farms in the area as part of the UNDP programme

Flocks and dogs gather to drink together on a hot July day in Haymana district

Altogether 30 puppies were placed with ten flocks belonging to six farms in the area: two males and one female per flock. They spent their first 3 months at Doğa Farm, where they were familiarized with sheep and goats. They were vaccinated, monitored, and fed on a balanced proprietary puppy food until old enough to be weaned on to the traditional *yal*-based diet received by working dogs.

The project leader reported in 2008 that most of the farmers had persevered with the scheme and that most of the dogs were still working in the area, although a few had died in accidents, for example on the road. Only one farmer had sold his puppies; otherwise compliance had been good and it was estimated that over the 2-year term of the programme about 20 wolf killings had been avoided by the use of these Kangal Dogs. It was also felt that media publicity for the scheme had increased awareness of this method of control, both within the area and beyond.

The changing rural scene

It is to be hoped that incentives like these will halt or at least slow the decline in village populations and in sheep farming in Anatolia. Over the 20 years from 1989 to 2009 sheep numbers in Turkey fell from 40 million to 25 million, in Sivas province from 400,000 to 250,000. In line with this, the rural population as a percentage of the total Turkish population fell from 40 to 25 per cent. This seems to be an inevitable trend as the country develops. In fact, the European Union wants this figure to be reduced to 10–15 per cent. In developed countries the urban population is over 85 per cent of the total population.

Economic development need not mean the end of sheep farming in the region. As is happening in south-eastern Turkey, farming in the Sivas-Kangal area may in future be carried out as agribusiness by large holdings, with higher yields and an integrated system of processing, sales and distribution. And Kangal Dogs will still be needed to guard the flocks. The extensive state farm at Ulaş near Sivas, for example, keeps more than 50 Kangals to protect its large flocks of sheep and for breeding.

Twin lambs on a productive farm near Havuz

A local initiative: the Kangal Akkaraman Sheep Project

This project aims to improve the quality of the local Kangal Akkaraman breed of sheep by encouraging the use of the best available rams for breeding purposes.

Over a 10-year period and using 10,000 sheep, the plan aims to raise the lambing rate. A number of farms with excellent rams have been selected to take part in this scheme, which is being carried out with the participation of the Veterinary Faculty of Selçuk University, Konya, and the Turkish State Planning Organization.

With increased lamb production the population of breeding sheep in the area will expand, creating a greater need for dogs to protect them. If the scheme is a success it will help to secure a future for the Kangal Dog in its traditional role.

Farms in the area carry a plaque to show that they are participants in the Kangal Akkaraman Sheep Project

Alternative roles for the Kangal Dog

It seems likely that in future there will be an increase in the number of Kangals being used in alternative roles, and in other countries. Dr Yusuf Oğrak of Cumhuriyet University, Sivas, believes that there are now (2009) greater numbers of Kangals worldwide than 20 years ago but they are carrying out different duties.

Watchdogs and companions

Over approximately the last 25 years the Kangal Dog has been 'discovered' by middle-class urbanites in Turkey. As they have increasingly moved from the luxury flats which were the residence of choice until the mid-1980s into villas set in gardens, they have found the need for a large dog to guard their property from the ubiquitous burglars. The Kangal, with its imposing physique and strong guarding instincts, is often chosen for this purpose. For the same reasons, Kangals are being used to guard industrial and commercial premises such as factories and warehouses in various parts of Turkey.

As a result, the commercial breeding of Kangals to supply this market has increased over recent years. This is now providing another source of income for the people of the Sivas/Kangal area. In addition to the state breeding establishments at Ulaş and Kangal town, and at Cumhuriyet University in Sivas, some private individuals have set up breeding kennels. High prices are often commanded by such breeders.

Kangals are seen as prestigious pets. As the 'national dog', Kangals are sometimes presented as gifts to important state visitors. Turkish president Abdullah Gül was presented with two Kangal puppies on a visit to the city of Sivas in 2008. Newspaper photos showed the delighted president patting his new acquisitions.

Military duties

The Turkish army has in the past attempted to train Kangals for military use, without much success. Doğan Kartay, a Kangal dog breeder and enthusiast in Turkey for over 50 years, ascribes this to faulty training methods that do not take into account the special character of the breed. Controversially, he still advocates using the dogs for military and police duties but he believes that, unlike most other breeds, Kangals cannot be trained with harsh treatment, strict commands or by using food as a reward. Instead, friendly handling and praise are what motivate a Kangal to co-operate (Kartay, 2007).

As Doğan Bey explains, Kangals tend to be loyal to one master for life, so for police or military duties it is essential that the dog is trained by and works with one master. However, soldiers in Turkey are normally conscripted for about 18 months and frequent changes of trainer confuse the dogs.

He also has a theory that training sessions should take place at night, since that is when the dogs are at their most alert. Finally he asserts that they should never be chained but be allowed to move freely in a large compound.

Mehmet, the kennel manager at the Keskinoğlu plant in Akhisar, with some of Doğan Kartay's dogs

Doğan Kartay

Izmir-born Doğan Kartay dates his interest in the Kangal Dog back to 1952, when he was assigned to do his military service in the Kangal district. As an engineer with the Turkish Ministry of Public Works he also spent the years 1963–1965 and 1978–1980 in the Sivas-Kangal region. During these years his interest in and contact with the breed increased and gradually came to dominate his life. Now in retirement, he raises Kangals on his farm near the village of Gökceler in the hills near Izmir, and has written a number of books and articles on the breed. Although interested in all Turkish shepherd dog breeds, he has devoted his life to the welfare of the Kangal Dog in particular.

In 2005 a disease outbreak among his dogs, possibly ehrlichiosis, forced Doğan Bey to find a temporary alternative home for his 70 Kangals while his farm was cleared of the infection. To the rescue came Ismail Keskinoğlu, who rehoused all the dogs at his family's large poultry farm at Akhisar, east of Izmir. Although he has a large number of dogs, Doğan Bey knows all their names and ancestry. The dogs all know him and greet him enthusiastically. Doğan Bey says the love and attention he has given to his Kangals over the years have cost him his marriages. But he doesn't seem to mind; the Kangal Dog is obviously his greatest love.

An international ambassador

During recent years there has been increasing interest abroad in using the Kangal Dog in its traditional role as a non-lethal deterrent for predator species. With a growing awareness of the importance of biodiversity, and as international concern develops for wildlife species under threat of extinction, there is a demand for methods of protecting livestock that are ecologically sustainable. The special skills of the Kangal fit perfectly into this picture.

Carefully bred young Kangal Dogs, from lines proven to work effectively with stock, could be good ambassadors for Turkey to countries around the world. The major obstacle to this, of course, is the government's veto on the export of Kangals. The Ministry of Culture's firm stance on this is perfectly understandable considering the history of dogs being shipped abroad and either crossed with other breeds or misrepresented in foreign registries. After all, for many years there was little appreciation among Western owners of the breed's special status in Turkey, and little interest in learning about it from the Turks themselves.

A young Kangal in Sweden, a descendant of expatriate Turkish ancestors

Many of the Kangals in countries outside Turkey are the descendants of dogs that were exported, or left the country with their owners, before the restriction came into force. As a result, foreign breeders are working with a very small gene pool. Breeding centres in the Sivas area are looking into the possibility of establishing a sperm bank, which might open the door for exportation of frozen semen to suitable recipients abroad without compromising the domestic population.

Research

Veterinary faculties at universities all over Turkey have conducted research into various aspects of Kangal Dogs, from heart function and reproductive characteristics to genetics. Most innovative among these research activities are the continuing DNA studies carried out at Middle East Technical University (METU) by Professor İnci Togan, Dr Evren Koban and their team. These researchers and the Veterinary Faculties of Istanbul University and Selçuk University, Konya, work closely with the Kangal Dog Breeding and Research Centre, which is based at Cumhuriyet University, Sivas, and has access to local populations of dogs for study.

The Kangal Dog Research and Breeding Centre

Kangal Dogs have been bred at Sivas Cumhuriyet University since October 2003, when the Kangal Dog Research and Breeding Centre was established to study health and development aspects of the breed, and as a conservation initiative. The Centre has a resident population of about 30 dogs but, being located at the heart of Kangal country, it also has access to large numbers of working dogs and their owners in the villages, and is well placed to monitor and report on the breed's situation on the ground.

Head of the research centre is Dr Yusuf Ziya Oğrak, a veterinarian and senior lecturer at the University who helped set up and design the facility. A Sivas man, Dr Oğrak has very good local knowledge and a long association with Kangal Dogs; he and his brother adopted a Kangal puppy when he was just 6 years old. He graduated with a Masters degree from Istanbul University and still maintains close links with the Veterinary Faculty there, as well as working closely with Erciyes University, Kayseri, Mustafa Kemal University, Antakya-Hatay, METU, and Tübitak, the Scientific and Technical Research Council of Turkey. Tübitak has supported and published a number of research studies involving Kangal Dogs. Dr Oğrak's own projects have included research into blood typing, reproductive traits and heart disease.

He feels strongly that the best way to safeguard the future of this unique regional breed is by gathering and disseminating knowledge about it. A breed standard must reflect not only the physical appearance of the dog but also

its behavioural characteristics. A good Kangal, he says, is one that fulfils the owner's needs as a working dog, by bonding with the stock and exhibiting the strong protective instinct for which the breed is famous.

Dr Oğrak with some of the Kangal Dogs at the research centre in Sivas

Threats to the breed

Perhaps the greatest threat to the continuation of the Kangal Dog as a recognizable, authentic breed is not ill health, loss of habitat or decline in sheep husbandry, but exploitation by people.

Cross-breeding for size

Since the Kangal Dog became well known worldwide in the late 20th century, attempts have been made to exaggerate some of the natural qualities and characteristics for which it is famous. This is a large, impressive breed, but there is always an element among animal breeders who feel that there is something to be gained from breeding for extremes. For some, the Kangal described in the breed standard agreed in 2005 is not enough. In an attempt to breed a bigger, heavier, more aggressive animal they have turned to the 'Malaklı' or 'Aksaray' mastiff-type dog that can be found in other areas of Turkey, notably the Konya region. The resulting hybrid is seen increasingly at Turkish breeding kennels and at shows: dogs with the classic Kangal markings, but with massive heads, pendulous jowls and the heavy leg bones and huge feet of the mastiff. Often even the characteristic curled tail and the double coat have been sacrificed in these breedings.

The mastiff-type head of the Malaklı dog is quite different from that of the Kangal

Dog fighting

The most disturbing abuse of this breed is its use in organized dog fighting in Turkey. As everyone knows, this is a sport that has continued throughout many centuries, not only in developing countries but in so-called civilized society, including Britain. It persists particularly in Eastern European and Asian countries, where dog fighting is a lucrative business in which large sums of money are wagered on tournaments often held before a mass audience.

Turkey is no exception. It is a regrettable fact that most of the major breeders of Kangals allow their strongest dogs to be used in fighting. Some will defend the practice by saying that it is traditional, or that no dogs are actually killed in these contests (there are deaths). Some will tell you that they used to be involved but no longer are, or that they only do the organizing, or that they only spectate. The truth is that there is a whole, well-orchestrated network of participants, some working covertly, others proclaiming their dogs' successes on placards at their kennels or on internet sites, and all underpinned by a system of corruption and racketeering.

There is a connection between dog fighting and the issue of interbreeding with the Malaklı mastiffs described above, for these are the dogs that make the most effective fighters. Kangal Dogs are by nature defensive rather than aggressive, and it takes human intervention to turn them into the kind of animal that will perform on the fight circuit. Besides cross-breeding for size and temperament, body-building steroids and other drugs are used; dogs are confined, goaded and teased to make them react more fiercely when threatened. One ploy used to produce a fierce response in a Kangal forced to take part in an organized fight was to place a child from its family in the ring near the dogs as they squared up to each other; this of course brought out the Kangal's strongest instinct, that of defending its own.

On 24 June 2004 the Turkish Grand National Assembly passed law number 5199, the Animal Protection Law. It covers all animals in Turkey, but there are certain provisions, including those concerning fighting, which particularly affect the treatment of dogs.

The Turkish Animal Protection Law
Law number 5199, passed on 24 June 2004

Article 1 of this law states that its purpose is:

To ensure that animals are afforded a comfortable life and receive good and proper treatment, to protect them in the best manner possible from the infliction of pain, suffering and torture, and to prevent all types of cruel treatment.

Of direct relevance to dog fighting, Article 11 states:

*It is forbidden to pit animals against other live animals. Traditional shows with folkloric value **which do not involve violence** may be organised by obtaining permission from the provincial animal welfare committee, with the approval of the ministry.*
(our emphasis)

In an echo of the Universal Declaration of Human Rights, the first fundamental principle of Law 5199 states:

All animals are born equal and have a right to life within the framework of the provisions of this law.

People concerned with animal welfare in Turkey have brought court cases under law 5199, for example against local authorities. However, the law has been described as 'without teeth' and criticized as unworkable in its current form. A group of lawyers in Istanbul is working to rectify this.

Stray dogs in Turkey

Law 5199 may in theory be among the best animal protection laws in the world. However, it is one thing to have the law on the statute book, it is another thing to implement and enforce it.

According to the law, stray domesticated animals are to be supported in the same way as animals with owners. Article 6 requires local authorities to capture, neuter and vaccinate stray animals and release them into the environment they were taken from. A number of these authorities already carry out this regime for street dogs rather than exterminating them as in the past. There are, however, still occasional reports of poisoning, and often the dogs are not released into their original environment, where they are usually known to local restaurants or residents who feed them. Unfamiliar dogs with new plastic tags on their ears turn up suddenly on the streets of city districts. And Kangal or part-Kangal dogs are sometimes among them.

The system aims to deal with the street dog population, a centuries-old problem in Turkish towns and cities. In 1911, for example, the governor of Istanbul ordered the stray dogs in the streets to be rounded up and deposited on Sivriada, one of the Princes' Islands in the Sea of Marmara. Apparently there was a severe earthquake immediately following this act, which was regarded as divine retribution for abandoning the animals.

The first prosecutions of fight organizers under this legislation are yet to be seen, however (2008). It may be hard to understand why enforcement has not followed. One view attributes this to pressures within Turkish society: whistle blowers are not popular; police officers who make arrests put themselves and their families at risk, if not of physical harm, then of social alienation for their family. A veterinarian who treats a dog with obvious fight damage and then reports it may cause another injured dog untold suffering from being patched up inexpertly rather than brought to the clinic. Until the legislation is actually implemented it remains no more than window dressing for the sake of public appeasement and the enhancement of Turkey's international image.

Pressure groups of dog lovers have been formed but to date their protests have been poorly co-ordinated and tend towards the histrionic.

Dog fighting is not only against the law, it goes against Moslem teachings. Among other forms of cruelty towards animals mentioned in the *hadith*s, organizing fights between animals is said to have been condemned by the Prophet Mohammed.

If the Kangal Dog is ever to achieve the respect it deserves on the world stage, the shadow of dog fighting has to be lifted. To take a firm, uncompromising stand against this barbaric practice will present Turkey as a humane, modern member of the international community.

The words of Mahatma Gandhi are as true today as they were 60 years ago:

> *The greatness of a nation and its moral progress can be judged by the way it treats its animals.*

The road ahead

The direction taken by this breed in the years to come will depend on many things. Turkey's developing economy may threaten the traditional way of life in the countryside, but at the same time the world is waking up to the need for sustainable ecosystems. The Kangal Dog still has a part to play in that delicate balance, at home and abroad.

Modern transport and infrastructure have opened up a region that was once barely accessible, improving the quality of life of many people and allowing outsiders a glimpse of the wonders of Anatolia. But has this also opened the door to exploitation? Sharing the Kangal Dog with the rest of the world has had good and bad results.

One thing is certain: knowledge about this very special breed is increasing all the time. The better our understanding, the more likely it is that the Kangal Dog will retain its unique role as protector, companion and friend.

References

Alderson, L. (1978) *A Chance to Survive: Rare breeds in a changing world.* London, Cameron & Tayleur

Altunok, V., Koban, E., Chikhi, L., Schaffer, A., Pedersen, N.C., Nizamlıoğlu, M. and Togan, İ. (2005) 'Genetic evidence for the distinctness of Kangal Dogs', Bulletin of the Veterinary Institute in Pulawy 49:249–54

Balsan, F. (1945) *The Sheep and the Chevrolet.* London, Paul Elek

Beresford-Ellis, P. (1990) *The Celtic Empire.* London, Constable

Bryce, T. (2002) *Life and Society in the Hittite World.* Oxford, Oxford University Press

Bryce, T. (2005) *The Kingdom of the Hittites.* Oxford, Oxford University Press

Buckland, F. (1863) 'Turkish guard dog from Trebizond', *The Field* 23 May: 501

Childs, W.J. (1917) *Across Asia Minor On Foot.* Edinburgh and London, William Blackwood & Sons

Coppinger, R., Coppinger, L., Langeloh, G., Gettler, L. and Lorenz, J. (1988) 'A decade of use of livestock guarding dogs', in *Proceedings of the Thirteenth Vertebrate Pest Conference.* Lincoln NA, University of Nebraska

Curtis, J. and Reade, J.E. (2005) *Art and Empire: Treasures from Assyria in the British Museum.* London, British Museum Press

Çağatay, E. and Kuban, D. (2006) *The Turkic Speaking Peoples.* Munich, Prestel Verlag

Çelebi, E. (1631–1670) *Seyahatname (Book of Travels)*

Dawydiak, O. and Sims, D.E. (2004) *Livestock Protection Dogs—Selection, care and training.* Loveland CO, Alpine

De Bernières, L. (2004) *Birds Without Wings.* London, Secker and Warburg

DeBroff, B.M. and Pahk, P.J. (2003) 'The ability of periorbitally applied antiglare products to improve contrast sensitivity in conditions of sunlight exposure', *Archives of Ophthalmology* **121**:97–101

Demirci, T. (2005) 'Owners' approaches to keeping Kangal Dogs—a clinician's view', in Oğrak, Y.Z. (ed.) *Proceedings of the 2nd International Kangal Dog Symposium.* Sivas, Kangal Governorship/Sivas Governorship/Cumhuriyet University

Dohner, J.V. (2007) *Livestock Guardians: Using dogs, donkeys and llamas to protect your herd.* North Adams MA, Storey

Fitzherbert, A. (1985) Personal communication

Frye, R. (2006) in Çağatay and Kuban (ibid.)

Hare, B., Brown, M., Williamson, C. and Tomasello, M. (2002) 'The domestication of social cognition in dogs', *Science* **298**:1634–6

Hare, B. and Tomasello, M. (2005) 'Human-like social skills in dogs?', *Trends in Cognitive Science* **9**(10):463–4

Hiçyılmaz, G. (1990) *Against the Storm.* New York, Viking

Houghton Brodrick, A. (1972) *Animals in Archaeology.* London, Barrie & Jenkins

Izady, M.R. (1993) 'Exploring Kurdish origins', *Kurdish Life* 7

Jenkins, D.J (2003) *Guard Animals for Livestock Protection: Existing and potential use in Australia.* Orange, New South Wales Department of Agriculture

Karadağ, H. (2002) 'An investigation on the opinions on the place name of Kangal and the origin of Kangal Dog', *Milli Folklor Dergisi* 7(56): 34–45

Karagöz, A. (2001, updated 2006) *Country Pasture/Forage Resource Profiles: Turkey*. Rome, Food and Agriculture Organization

Kartay, D. (2007) *Bozkırın Gözcüsü Türk Çoban Köpeği 'Kangal'*. Ankara, T.C. Kültür Bakanlığı Yayınları

Koban, E., Gökçek Saraç, Ç., Açan, S.C., Savolainen, P. and Togan, İ. (2008) 'Genetic relationship between Kangal, Akbash and other dog populations', *Discrete Applied Mathematics* 157(10): 335–40

Lancaster, R. (1977) 'Ten days in Turkey', *The Garden*, December

Macqueen, J.G. (1975, 2001) *The Hittites*. London, Thames & Hudson

Marker, L.L. (2005) 'Evaluating the effectiveness of livestock guarding dogs as a method of conflict resolution', in Oğrak (ed.) (ibid.)

Mellaart, J. (1999) 'Under the volcano', *Cornucopia* 4(19):76–99

Ministry of Culture and Tourism (2008) *Ankara and the Central Anatolian Region*. Ankara, Ministry of Culture and Tourism

Morris, D. (2001) *Dogs: The ultimate dictionary of over 1000 dog breeds*. London, Ebury Press

Murray, M. and Njogu, A.R. (1989) 'African trypanosomiasis in wild and domestic ungulates: the problem and its control', *Symposia of the Zoological Society of London* 61:218–21

Nadel, B. (2006) *Dance With Death*. London, Headline

Oğrak, Y.Z. (ed.) (2005) *Proceedings of the 2nd International Kangal Dog Symposium*. Sivas, Kangal District Governorship/Sivas Governorship/Cumhuriyet University

Onar, V., Armutak, A., Belli, O. and Konyar, E. (2002) 'Skeletal remains of dogs unearthed from the Van-Yoncatepe necropolises', *International Journal of Osteoarchaeology* 12:317–34

Öncül, O. (1983) Sadık Dostumuz Köpekler Ailesi (The Dog Family: Our faithful friend). Ankara, Dönmez

Özcan, M., Yılmaz, A. and Oğrak, Y.Z. (2005) 'The breed standard of the Kangal Dog', in Oğrak (ed.) (ibid.)

Özdemir, A., (2006) *Ergenekon Destanı*. Istanbul, Bordo Siyah

Payne, S. (1984) Personal communication

Pumpelly, R. (1908) *Explorations in Turkestan, Expedition of 1904: Prehistoric civilizations of Anau, origins, growth and influence of environment*. Washington DC, Carnegie Institution

Rålamb, C. (1658) *Costume Book*

Rigg, R. (2001) *Livestock Guarding Dogs: Their current use worldwide*, IUCN/SSC Canid Specialist Group Occasional Paper No. 1. Gland, International Union for the Conservation of Nature/Species Survival Commission (IUCN/SSC)

Rigg, R. (2005) *Livestock Guarding Dogs and Carnivore Conservation: A new role for an old tradition*. Liptovsky Hrádok, Slovak Wildlife Society

Savolainen, P., Zhang, Y., Luo, J., Lundeberg, J. and Leitner, T. (2002) 'Genetic evidence for an East Asian origin of domestic dogs', *Science* 298:1610–13

Sponenberg, D.P. (1998) 'Livestock guard dogs: What is a breed, and why does it matter?', *Akbash Sentinel* 44:13–17

Talbot Rice, T. (1961) *The Seljuks*. London, Thames & Hudson

Taylor, T. (1996) 'Breeding of Turkish shepherd dogs in America', in *Proceedings of the International Symposium on Turkish Shepherd Dogs*. Konya, Selçuk University Veterinary Faculty

Tekinşen, O.C. (1996) Personal communication

Türk Standardlar Enstitüsü (1997) *Damızlık Hayvanlar—Kangal Köpeği (Breeding Stock—Kangal Dog)*, TS 12172. Ankara, Turkish Standards Institute

UNDP Global Environment Facility (GEF) (2006) *Protection of Wildlife through Use of Kangal Shepherd Dogs in Traditional Animal Husbandry* (TUR-03-11). New York, GEF Small Grants Programme

Vilà, C., Savolainen, P., Maldonado, J.E., Amorim, I.R., Rice, J.E., Honeycutt, R.L. *et al.* (1997) 'Multiple and ancient origins of the domestic dog', *Science* 276(5319):1687–9

Walker, W.S. and Uysal, A.E. (1966) 'The Kadi and "Karabash"', in *Tales Alive in Turkey*. Cambridge MA, Harvard University Press

World Meteorological Organization (2009) *1961–1990 Global Climate Normals*. Asheville NC, National Climatic Data Center (US)

World Small Animal Veterinary Association (WSAVA) (2007) 'Guidelines for the vaccination of dogs and cats', *Journal of Small Animal Practice* 48:528–41

Yalçin, B.C. (1986) *Sheep and Goats in Turkey*, FAO Animal Production and Protection Paper 60. Rome, Food and Agriculture Organization

Yılmaz, O. (2007) *Turkish Kangal (Karabash) Shepherd Dog*. Istanbul, O. Yılmaz

Photography

Chapter opening photographs

Chapter 1 *Introducing the Kangal Dog*
Yiğido the Kangal surveys a wintry Sivas landscape
by Yusuf Ziya Oğrak

Chapter 2 *The historical setting*
This 4000-year-old relief of a lion hunt was excavated at
Alacahöyük, near Hattusas, capital of the Hittite Empire
by Margaret Mellor

Chapter 3 *Origins*
A timeless scene in Kirghizstan: nomadic pastoralists with
their sheep on the Central Asian steppe
by Ergun Çağatay

Chapter 4 *Nature, adaptation, type*
Zalım, Zülüm and Karabaş follow their flock to the upland
pastures at Doymuş hamlet
by Lesley Tahtakılıç

Chapter 5 *Kangals at work*
Kangal Dogs amid their flock near Kargakalesi at the end
of a long day
by Öykü Yağcı

Chapter 6 *Life in Kangal country*
Puppies make their debut at the Kangal Festival,
highlight of the year in Kangal district
by courtesy of Kangal Kaymakamlığı

Chapter 7 *Kangals abroad*
In Sweden, Shayan the Kangal and her young friend Robin
share a quiet moment in the woods
by Susanne Edlund

Chapter 8 *Identity*
A national icon, Samsun the Kangal Dog takes part in
the celebration of Turkish Children's Day (23 April) in
Raleigh, North Carolina
by Susan Kocher

Chapter 9 *Health, care and ownership*
Lucy and her littermates take turns for their regular
cuddle on the Lamberts' farm in California
by Kathy Lambert

Chapter 10 *The future*
Working Kangals Tomi and Ateş carry out their traditional
role in Turkey
by Mustafa Sönmezer

Photo credits

All other photographs are by the authors.

Acknowledgements

The authors would like to thank the following people and organizations who contributed information for this book.

The people of Sivas province, for telling us about their lives, history and dogs
Dr Yusuf Ziya Oğrak, without whose help, patience and local knowledge our research would not have been possible

Ankara Zoo
Dean Baylis, British Museum
Cornucopia
Ergun Çağatay and Doğan Kuban
Louis de Bernières
The families of Doymuş hamlet
Susanne Edlund
The Field
Anthony Fitzherbert
The Garden/Royal Horticultural Society
HAYTAP Hayvan Hakları Federasyonu
Dr Charmian Hussey
Islamic Affairs Office, Istanbul
The Kangal Dog Club of America
Kangal Kaymakamlığı
Turhan Kangal
Onur Kanlı

Doğan Kartay
İsmail Keskinoğlu
Susan Kocher and KAPSI (Kangal–Akbash Preservation Society International)
Let's Adopt!/Sahip Çıkalım
James and Alan Mellaart
Professor Mustafa Özcan and Professor Vedat Onar, Istanbul University
Dr Sebastian Payne
Maureen Rose
Drs Arda and İrem Sancak
Dr Phillip Sponenberg
Tolga Tem
Nihal Tırpan, Museum of Anatolian Civilizations, Ankara
İlker Ünlü
İnci Willard

About the authors

Lesley Tahtakılıç is a freelance writer mainly dealing with aspects of life in Turkey. After graduating from Auckland University, New Zealand, with a BA in English Literature, she worked as a teacher and teacher trainer for over 30 years before taking up freelance writing. As a lifelong dog lover she quickly became aware of the existence of the Kangal Dog after moving to Turkey in 1972, but it was not until she was asked to take care of two Kangal puppies en route from Ankara Zoo to the United Kingdom that she had hands-on experience of the breed. During the weekend of their stay she and her Turkish husband fell in love with the dogs and were determined to have one of their own. After moving to a Bosphorus village near open countryside they were lucky enough to obtain their first Kangal from Sivas in 1982. They have been devoted to the breed ever since then.

Margaret Mellor is a British freelance editor working mainly in higher education. After a commercial training as a translator she worked in London, first for an international company as deputy editor of its multilanguage journals, and later in precious metals trading. It was after moving with her husband to Bedfordshire that she met Selim, a large, fawn, black-faced puppy bred in England from a dog imported from Ankara Zoo. So began a lasting admiration for the breed that she later came to know as the Kangal Dog. The Mellors have now owned Kangals for nearly 30 years. Margaret is a frequent traveller in Turkey, a regular visitor to Sivas, and a campaigner for the worldwide conservation of the Kangal Dog as a very special breed.

Index